NEXT-LEVEL SKILLS

12 WEEKS TO THINK SHARPER, LEAD SMARTER, AND COMMUNICATE WITH IMPACT

A practical playbook
to accelerate
your mindset, influence,
and professional growth

ABHISHEK SHARMA

This edition first self-published in 2025 in Australia.
Typeset in 12/14 pt Georgia.

© Abhishek Sharma
The moral rights of the author have been asserted.

A catalogue record for this book is available both from the National Library of Australia and State Library NSW.

All rights reserved. Except as permitted under the *Australian Copyright Act 1968* (for example, fair dealing for the purposes of study, research, criticism, or review), no part of this book may be reproduced, stored in a retrieval system, communicated, or transmitted in any form or by any means without prior written permission from the author.

ISBN: 978-1-7644138-5-5

Disclaimer
The material in this publication is of the nature of general comment only and does not represent professional advice. It is not intended to provide specific guidance for particular circumstances and should not be relied upon as the basis for any decision to take action or not to take action on any matter covered. Readers should obtain professional advice where appropriate before making any such decision. To the maximum extent permitted by law, the author and the publisher disclaim all responsibility and liability to any person arising directly or indirectly from any person taking or not taking action based on the information in this publication.

Contents

This book is dedicated to all individuals committed to achieving their Next-Level of excellence.

Next-Level Skills

Contents

Contents 5
Preface 7
Introduction: The Journey from Chaos to Clarity ... 11
Part I – The Inner Foundation: Mastering Self 17
Chapter 1: Self Awareness 21
Chapter 2: Emotional Intelligence 51
Chapter 3: Active Listening 79
Part II – The Adaptive Mindset: Thriving in Change
.... 105
Chapter 4: Adaptability 109
Chapter 5: Strategic Thinking 137
Chapter 6: Clear Communication 165
Part III – The Human Connection: Building Trust and Collaboration 191
Chapter 7: Conflict Resolution 195
Chapter 8: Accountability 221
Chapter 9: Leadership Without Authority 249
Part IV – The Growth Continuum: Sustaining Purpose and Impact 277
Chapter 10: Resilience 281
Chapter 11: Personal Goal Setting 307
Chapter 12: Storytelling for Influence 333

Next-Level Skills

Chapter 13: Integration – Bringing It All Together *359*

Epilogue – The Journey Continues *373*

Next Steps – Putting It into Practice *375*

Book Immediately *381*

Appendix I – Tools and Practices *397*

Appendix II – Next-Level Skills Planner *401*

Looking Ahead Together! *413*

About the Author *415*

References *417*

Index *453*

Preface

At the beginning of my career, I believed that being successful meant working quickly and efficiently.

Over time, I discovered that real progress is achieved not just through speed, but by connecting with others and understanding their perspectives.

As I continued my professional journey, forming strong relationships and adapting to new circumstances became equally as vital as completing tasks.

I deeply realised that the toughest obstacles were less about systems or schedules and more about developing skills – skills that everyone has the potential to learn.

Human skills.

Skills that help you navigate uncertainty, understand others, stay calm under pressure, and lead with clarity and empathy.

That realisation sparked *Next-Level Skills* – a "ready-to-apply" framework born from practice, reflection, and years of working across diverse teams, cultures, countries and industries.

This book focuses on practical strategies for self-transformation, sharing methods that have helped me, and many others achieve real change through commitment.

You will find that each chapter presented in this book, serves as a step, moving from increased self-awareness to integrating all skills together to have a greater influence on your surroundings.

The emphasis remains on actionable techniques to help you progress steadily to the Next-Level of your personal and professional growth, irrespective of the profession you are in.

Preface

The timing of when you choose to progress to each subsequent next step is entirely at your discretion.

Although this book is structured for a weekly schedule, it can be adapted for fortnightly, or even monthly intervals according to your preference.

The key is to keep moving forward.

Progress at your own pace. This book is designed to accommodate your individual learning speed.

You'll find ideas, stories, and practical exercises that you can apply immediately – whether you've just started your professional journey, working already in an individual contributor role, started to lead a team, already managing a growing team and the challenges that come as byproduct, managing clients or customers, or simply managing to better yourself.

No matter your situation, this book is here to support you *with practical ways*!

Next-Level Skills

I strongly believe that in a world that's changing faster than ever, *technical skills may open doors – but human skills keep them open.*

If this book helps you lead with more clarity, communicate with more purpose, and grow with more confidence, then its mission is certainly fulfilled.

Welcome to your Next-Level!

Abhishek Sharma,
Author, Next-Level Skills

Introduction: The Journey from Chaos to Clarity

We live in a world that rewards speed – yet demands *depth*.

Emails, deadlines, and deliverables pull us in every direction, while the skills that matter most – **empathy, adaptability, and influence** – often get buried under piles of those so-called urgencies.

As I navigated through the whirlwind of my own professional experiences, juggling emails, deadlines, and a never-ending stream of deliverables, a profound realisation dawned on me.

It's not more busy professionals that the world is crying out for. Instead, what's truly needed are individuals who can cut through the noise – those who bring genuine order to chaos and create meaning where there's only motion.

This insight became the cornerstone of my journey, shaping the direction of this book and the skills I believe we all need to truly thrive.

More than anything, world now needs self-aware, emotionally intelligent, adaptable leaders – people who can bring order to complexity and meaning to motion.

And that's what this book is about.

Introduction: The Journey from Chaos to Clarity

Next-Level Skills is structured as a journey of transformation in four parts, tailored to your own set pace:

Part I: You begin with **self** – mastering awareness, emotion, and listening.

Part II: You evolve through **adaptability** and **strategic clarity** – thinking bigger, acting smarter.

Part III: You learn to **collaborate and lead** – even without authority.

Part IV: And finally, you sustain growth through **resilience**, **focus**, and **storytelling** – so your work doesn't just succeed, it *inspires!*

This journey will help you build on your existing strengths and guide you to reach your *Next-Level*.

Next-Level Skills

Part I
The Inner Foundation: Mastering Self
Growth begins within

CHAPTER 1	CHAPTER 2	CHAPTER 3
Self-Awareness	**Emotional Intelligence**	**Active Listening**
The Foundation Of Every Next-Level Skill	*The Skill That Amplifies Every Other One*	*The Hidden Power Behind Every Great Conversation*

Part II
The Adaptive Mindset: Thriving in Change
Flexibility is the modern superpower

CHAPTER 4	CHAPTER 5	CHAPTER 6
Adaptability	**Strategic Thinking**	**Clear Communication**
The Art of Staying Steady When Everything Changes	*Seeing the Forest and the Trees*	*Turning Vision into Understanding*

Part III
The Human Connection: Building Trust and Collaboration
Relationships are the real currency of leadership

CHAPTER 7	CHAPTER 8	CHAPTER 9
Conflict Resolution	**Accountability**	**Leadership Without Authority**
Turning Friction into Forward Motion	*Owning the Outcome – Not Just the Effort*	*Influence Without a Title*

Part IV
The Growth Continuum: Sustaining Purpose and Impact
True growth is built on resilience, clarity, and meaning

CHAPTER 10	CHAPTER 11	CHAPTER 12
Resilience	**Personal Goal Setting**	**Storytelling for Influence**
Bending Without Breaking	*Direction Over Distraction*	*Turning Insight into Impact*

CHAPTER 13
Integration – Bringing It All Together

From Learning to Living

Introduction: The Journey from Chaos to Clarity

Every chapter in each of the four parts, combines practical insights and ideas, some real-world examples, and guided reflection.

Because growth isn't built in a single breakthrough but resides in the continuum of consistent reflection and deliberate practice.

This isn't a manual. It's a mirror.

You'll also find a *"Take It Further"* section at the end of each chapter – your personal thinking space to apply, challenge, and deepen what you've learned.

In addition, every chapter includes a *"Chapter Immediately"* section highlighting a single-page chapter summary for quick reference.

Every week or fortnight or month (work at your own pace!), focus on improving upon one skill each from chapters 1–12, then use chapter 13 to bring all the skills together.

Next-Level Skills

Embrace this *self-paced* transformational journey — from chaos to clarity — as you move up towards *your Next-Level*.

So, take a deep breath.

And let's begin the journey!

Part I – The Inner Foundation: Mastering Self

Before we can lead others, we must first learn to lead ourselves.

Every project, every relationship, every breakthrough begins within – in the space where thoughts, feelings, and choices meet.

That's where clarity takes root.

Too often, we rush to manage circumstances before understanding our own patterns.

But real growth doesn't start with control – it starts with *consciousness, self-awareness*.

Next-Level Skills

Part I of this book — *The Inner Foundation: Mastering Self* — is about slowing down long enough to listen inward.

It's where awareness replaces autopilot, and reflection replaces reaction.

In the next three chapters, we'll explore how to know yourself more deeply (*Self-Awareness*), understand and manage emotions (*Emotional Intelligence*), and connect with others through genuine presence (*Active Listening*).

These aren't just soft skills — they're stability skills.

Because when you build a strong inner foundation, everything you do on the outside becomes stronger too. Isn't it?

PART I
The Inner Foundation: Mastering Self

01   **Self-Awareness**
The Foundation Of Every Next-Level Skill

02   **Emotional Intelligence**
The Skill That Amplifies Every Other One

03   **Active Listening**
The Hidden Power Behind Every Great Conversation

"Growth begins within"

Next-Level Skills

Chapter 1: Self Awareness

"The Foundation Of Every Next-Level Skill"

Next-Level Skills

"Seeing Yourself Clearly"

When a senior project leader at a fintech startup, received feedback that her *"leadership style felt intimidating,"* she was stunned. She saw herself as driven, not domineering.

After sitting down with her team, she realised her quick-fire communication and constant focus on deadlines were creating pressure, that she didn't intend, ever! Clearly, it wasn't her competence that needed fine-tuning – it was her *awareness* of how she showed up.

That week, she began journalling after meetings:
What energy did I bring into the room?
How did people respond?

Within a month, her relationships shifted. People felt heard, she felt lighter, and her team's performance improved.

The change wasn't about new tools or training.
It began with one thing: **self-awareness**.

Chapter 1: Self Awareness

As *Daniel Goleman*, a pioneer in emotional intelligence, puts it:

"Self-awareness is the ability to monitor our own emotions and reactions."

And that's where the journey to our Next-Level starts — with the courage to look inward before you look outward.

True growth begins when you choose to reflect on your own patterns, strengths, and hiccups, rather than blaming circumstances or others.

This honest self-examination not only clears the path for personal development but also sets a powerful example for your team.

By embracing the discomfort of an honest self-reflection, you unlock the ability to lead with authenticity and inspire those around you to do the same.

Next-Level Skills

"Why Self-Awareness Matters"

If there's one universal truth, that applies to personal and professional growth too, it's this: you can't manage what you don't understand – and that includes *yourself*.

Self-awareness is the cornerstone of every skill in this book. Without it, emotional intelligence becomes guesswork, leadership becomes accidental, and communication becomes one-sided.

At its core, self-awareness is your ability to recognise your emotions, triggers, strengths, blind spots, and the ripple effect you create in others.

It's not about being self-critical – it's about being *self-honest*, at the core.

Developing self-awareness isn't just about personal growth – it's a critical skill that influences leadership, decision-making, and emotional intelligence.

Chapter 1: Self Awareness

Here's why being self-aware is essential:

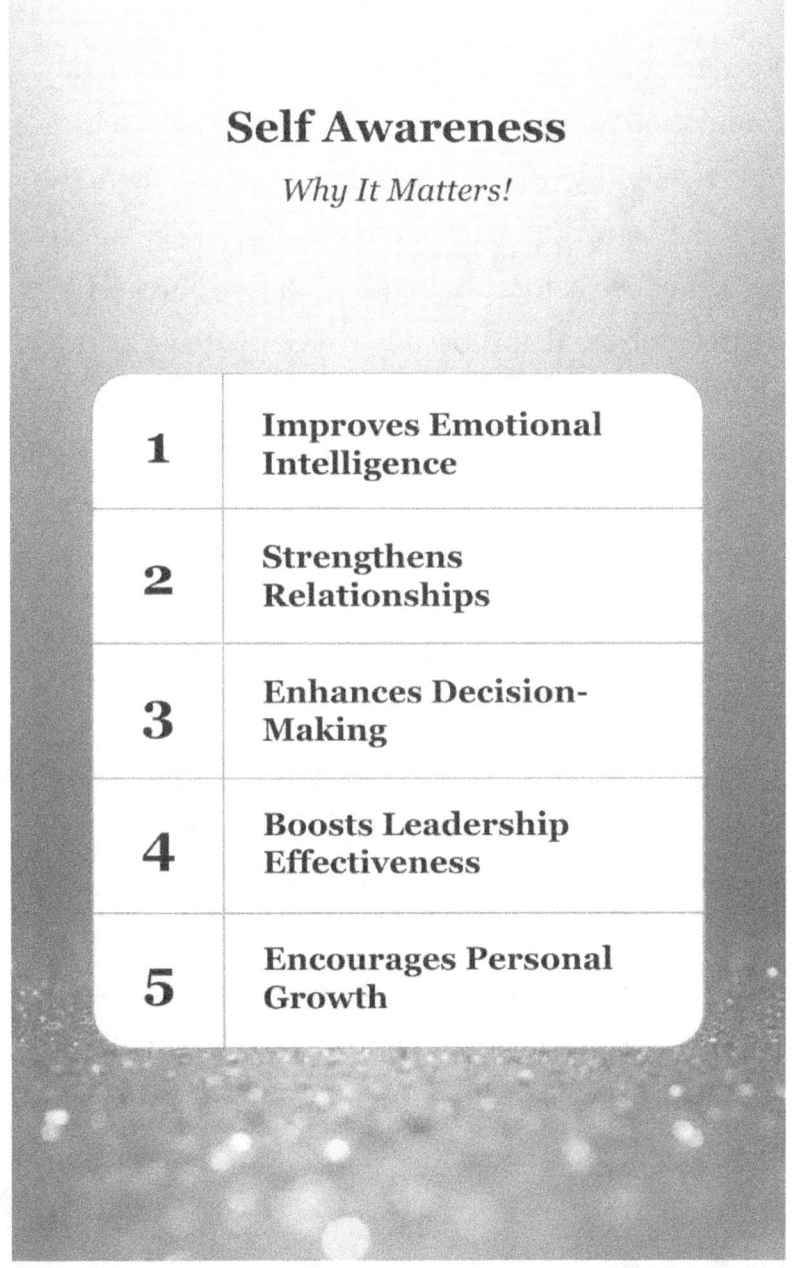

Improves Emotional Intelligence

Recognising and understanding our emotions is the foundation for emotional intelligence. When we're able to identify what we're feeling in the moment, we gain the power to regulate our reactions. This means we can pause before responding, choose our words deliberately, and approach situations with empathy and patience. Over time, this skill helps us avoid impulsive outbursts and make choices that align with our values, even when under stress or pressure. We will delve into this important skill in detail in the next chapter.

Strengthens Relationships

A clear sense of self-awareness helps us understand not only our own communication style but also how it's received by others. When we notice the effect our words and actions have on teammates, friends, and family, we can adjust our approach to foster trust and openness. This leads to more meaningful, productive, and harmonious interactions. By taking responsibility for our part in any exchange, we lay the groundwork for stronger connections and fewer misunderstandings, in the process.

Enhances Decision-Making

Self-aware people can spot their own personal biases, preferences, and blind spots, easily. This awareness enables them to take a step back, pause, consider different perspectives, and evaluate situations more objectively. As a result, their decisions are less likely to be swayed by hidden agendas or outbursts of sudden emotional reactions and more likely to be thoughtful, fair, and well-considered. Ultimately, this leads to better outcomes for themselves and for others who they interact with.

Boosts Leadership Effectiveness

Effective leaders possess a deep knowledge of their own strengths, weaknesses, and the way their behaviour influences those around them. By honestly assessing how they inspire, motivate, or even challenge others, leaders can adapt their style to get the best out of their team. This self-awareness creates a culture of trust and respect, where feedback is welcomed and everyone feels empowered to grow.

Encourages Personal Growth

Self-awareness provides a clear view of our own limitations, recurring patterns, and areas for development. When we're honest with ourselves about where we excel and where we struggle, we can set realistic goals and actively seek new learning opportunities. This habit of reflection helps us adapt to challenges, bounce back from setbacks, and continually improve both personally and professionally.

Organisational psychologist **Tasha Eurich** found that while 95% of people believe they're self-aware, only 10–15% are, really! She documented her findings in her Harvard Business Review article, "What Self-Awareness Really Is (and How to Cultivate It)" (2018), if you are interested in exploring this further.

That gap explains why so many talented professionals plateau – they're perhaps working hard, but not necessarily on the *right* things.

When you cultivate self-awareness, everything else accelerates. You make clearer decisions under pressure. You manage conflict with more composure. You learn faster because you know where you stumble.

And most importantly – you earn *trust*.

In my experience and understanding, humans can sense when someone truly knows themselves.

Understanding how much self-awareness matters, I know what are you now thinking about:

How do I build this in real life?

So, let's get right into some practical steps to develop this skill.

Next-Level Skills

"Practical Ways to Build Self Awareness"

Self-awareness grows through consistent reflection, observation, and curiosity.

"Self-awareness is not just about knowing ourselves – it's about understanding how we affect others"

Here's where awareness turns into daily practice – not mere theory. Try these six practical steps that has worked in real life for me and many others (*and not just in leadership seminars!*)

Step 1: Write Your Personal "User Manual"

Imagine you're onboarding yourself. Write a one-page guide titled *"How to Work with Me."*

Include the following in your one pager guide:

- *My strengths:* what energises me most
- *My derailers:* what frustrates me or shuts me down
- *My communication style:* how I prefer to give and receive information
- *My pressure triggers:* situations that make me reactive
- *My growth focus:* what I'm currently working on

This exercise brings structure to self-knowledge. It's surprisingly disarming to share it with a close colleague – it signals openness and sets expectations early.

Next-Level Skills

Step 2: Seek Real Feedback (Without Defending It)

Pick three to five people you trust – ideally a mix of peers, managers, and team members – and ask them:

> "What's one thing I do that makes collaborating with me easier?"

> "What's one thing I do that makes it harder?"

The key is to *listen*, not justify, under any circumstance whatsoever.

Always keep in mind, if you explain every piece of feedback, you'll train people not to give it again.

Receiving unfiltered insight is uncomfortable let alone uncommon – but that discomfort is the data, you need the most. So, keep it coming your way, always!

Step 3: Pause Before You React

Every time you feel an emotional surge – anger, frustration, defensiveness – take a breath and ask yourself:

> "What emotion am I actually feeling?"

> "What outcome do I want right now?"

A brief pause – though it may last only three seconds – effectively *distinguishes impulsive reactions from intentional responses.* The pause breaks the moment of high running emotions down and lets you recenter – to your wiser yourself. Over time, this practice fosters more composed leadership, particularly in high-pressure situations.

Undoubtedly, taking a moment before addressing significant or complex issues can yield positive results.

Intentional pauses promote thoughtful decision-making, often resulting in more substantive and constructive outcomes.

Step 4: Audit Your Energy

At the end of each day, jot down two simple lists:

When you felt *energised*

When you felt *drained*

Within a week, you'll notice patterns. Those clues help you design your work around your strengths and mitigate what depletes you.

Step 5: Clarify Your Core Values

List your top three personal values – **the non-negotiables.** They might be *growth, integrity, creativity, balance,* or *impact.*

Then, each evening, ask:

> *"Did I live my values today?"*

When your behaviour aligns with your values, you feel grounded. When it doesn't, you'll sense friction.

That awareness is a compass for course correction.

Step 6: Schedule Reflection Time Like a Meeting (with Yourself!)

Block 15 minutes every Friday to review your week.

Ask yourself:

> What did I learn about myself this week?

> When did I feel at my best?

> What triggered me?

This simple rhythm keeps awareness alive – not just an exercise you do once and forget.

Each of these steps is small, but together they build the quiet confidence of someone who understands themselves – and therefore, can lead others better.

Now, let's bring these concepts to life through the stories of people who've mastered (*and sometimes struggled with*) self-awareness in action.

Skill in action: Some real-world examples

Satya Nadella's Leadership Transformation at Microsoft

When Satya Nadella took the helm at Microsoft in 2014, the company had lost its innovative edge. The culture had hardened into internal competition and defensiveness, and the once-bold organisation was struggling to adapt.

Nadella realised early on that revitalising Microsoft wasn't only about technology – it was about *mindset.* His own journey of self-awareness, spurred by raising a son with special needs, had deepened his empathy and broadened his perspective on what leadership could mean.

He began by asking his senior team to read *Nonviolent Communication* and reflect on how they approached conflict. Under his leadership, "*know-it-alls*" became "*learn-it-alls.*" A needed mindset shift.

He often said that curiosity, humility, and empathy were not soft skills – they were *power skills*. Nadella's ability to first understand himself, his triggers, and his blind spots allowed him to reshape Microsoft's culture from within. His transformation as a person became the blueprint for the company's rebirth.

Awareness begins where ego ends

Oprah Winfrey and Conscious Self-Reflection

For decades, Oprah Winfrey has lived in front of the world – interviewing, performing, sharing, and listening. Yet, behind the camera, her most consistent practice has been solitude and self-reflection.

Every evening, she journals about what brought her joy, what tested her patience, and what lessons surfaced during the day. This private act of writing keeps her connected to her values amid the chaos of fame and influence.

When her show ended, she admitted she never once walked onto stage unprepared emotionally. Each episode was a lesson in awareness – of her guests, of the audience she faced, and of her own presence.

That emotional honesty translated into an unmatched connection with millions. Oprah's practice shows that success doesn't erase the need for reflection. *It amplifies it.*

Self-awareness turns experience into wisdom.

Ray Dalio's Radical Transparency at Bridgewater

When Ray Dalio founded Bridgewater Associates, he envisioned a place where truth would triumph over hierarchy. Over time, he realised that most workplaces suffer not from bad intentions but from blind spots – unexamined habits, hidden egos, and unspoken fears.

To counter that, he built what he called a "radically transparent" culture. Employees rated each other openly in meetings, shared feedback publicly, and discussed mistakes without shame. It was uncomfortable, even painful, but Dalio believed that self-awareness – both individual and collective – was the only path to real excellence.

This approach forced everyone, including Dalio himself, to confront their biases. He viewed criticism as a mirror, not a weapon. What began as a workplace experiment evolved into a personal philosophy: *if you can't see yourself clearly, you can't lead effectively.* Radical transparency made reflection a daily discipline, not an occasional event.

Transparency accelerates awareness.

Serena Williams and the Power of Honest Reflection

After losing the 2016 US Open, Serena Williams gave one of her most candid interviews. She admitted that her greatest opponent wasn't another player – it was her own frustration. In those moments of defeat, she learned to step back and ask,

Chapter 1: Self Awareness

"What's really happening inside me?"

That question turned self-critique into self-inquiry. Serena's success over two decades came not only from physical mastery but from her ability to separate emotion from identity, and performance from worth.

Off the court, she has spoken openly about balancing motherhood, ambition, and vulnerability. Her willingness to confront her emotions head-on allowed her to evolve without losing her edge.

In a sport defined by precision, Serena's greatest precision came from within – the discipline to look inward and realign before she returned to play.

"Reflection transforms reaction into growth"

Next-Level Skills

Howard Schultz's Listening Tour at Starbucks

In 2008, Starbucks was in trouble – stores were closing, morale was low, and its signature experience had become mechanical. When founder Howard Schultz returned as CEO, he resisted the instinct to issue directives. Instead, he went on what he called a "listening tour," visiting baristas, store managers, and customers across continents.

He asked questions more than he gave answers, sitting quietly as people described what had been lost.

Those conversations revealed something deeper than operational inefficiency: Starbucks had lost its sense of *why*.

Schultz later said the trip was less about fixing the business and more about rediscovering himself as a leader – the curious, idealistic young man who once believed coffee could build community.

Chapter 1: Self Awareness

Through listening, he re-anchored the company to its purpose and revived its culture of connection.

"Awareness grows strongest through listening"

These stories show that self-awareness isn't reserved for global CEOs or world leaders. It's a daily discipline – whether you're leading a nation, a team, or just yourself through a challenging project.

So, how can you internalise this for your own journey? It just comes down to 2 words, simply.

Reflection and action.

Next-Level Skills

Weekly Reflection Exercise

Take a quiet 10 minutes to reflect on these:

What emotions or patterns have I noticed most this week and what might they be telling me?

How do I think others perceive my leadership or communication style and what evidence supports that?

What situation recently triggered me, and how might I handle it differently next time?

Reflection isn't indulgent. It's an investment in clarity.

Chapter 1: Self Awareness

One Key Action Step This week

Ask one trusted colleague for *specific* feedback on your impact. Listen, take notes, and thank them – no explanations, no defences, no nothing!

Then reflect:

What did I learn about myself that I didn't know before?

You'll likely uncover something subtle but powerful – a blind spot, a strength you've overlooked, or a pattern ready to evolve.

More importantly, a way to move forward to your Next-Level!

Next-Level Skills

Final Reflection

Self-awareness isn't about perfection – it's about presence.

It's the *quiet skill that amplifies every other one*: emotional intelligence, adaptability, communication, leadership and many more!

The most effective professionals don't just *do* more.

They *notice* more – about themselves, their impact, and the world around them.

And that awareness?

That's where true growth begins!

As *Carl Jung* famously said,

"Until you make the unconscious conscious, it will direct your life, and you will call it fate."

Chapter 1: Self Awareness

Chapter Immediately

Self-Awareness

WHY IT MATTERS!

- ⭐ Improves Emotional Intelligence
- ⭐ Strengthens Relationships
- ⭐ Enhances Decision-Making
- ⭐ Boosts Leadership Effectiveness
- ⭐ Encourages Personal Growth

PRACTICAL WAYS TO BUILD THE SKILL

1. Write Your Personal "User Manual"

2. Seek Real Feedback (Without Defending It)

3. Pause Before You React

4. Audit Your Energy

5. Clarify Your Core Values

6. Schedule Reflection Time Like a Meeting (with Yourself!)

Next-Level Skills

Take It Further ...

- *How does regular reflection shape the way you respond to challenges at work or in your personal life?*

- *In what ways can self-awareness help you identify blind spots or biases you may hold?*

- *How do you distinguish between your own values and those influenced by others in your decision-making?*

- *What daily practices support you in becoming more attuned to your reactions and thought patterns?*

- *How can self-awareness foster empathy and understanding within your team or community?*

- *What are some signs that you might be ignoring important feedback, and how can you stay open to it?*

Chapter 1: Self Awareness

- *How do you ensure that your self-awareness leads to positive action, rather than just self-critique?*

- *How do you notice when your habits or routines are no longer serving your personal or professional growth?*

- *In what situations do you find it most challenging to remain self-aware, and how do you bring yourself back to a place of presence?*

- *What role does self-awareness play in helping you adapt to unexpected changes or setbacks, and how do you leverage this awareness to navigate uncertainty?*

Next-Level Skills

Chapter 2: Emotional Intelligence

"The Skill That Amplifies Every Other One"

Next-Level Skills

Building on the foundation of Self-Awareness,

Emotional Intelligence (EI) takes that inner clarity and turns it outward – into how we connect, influence, and collaborate with others.

If self-awareness is the mirror, emotional intelligence is the bridge.

It's what helps us stay composed under pressure, respond thoughtfully instead of reactively, and lead with empathy even when things get messy.

Chapter 2: Emotional Intelligence

"Understanding Before Being Understood"

A senior consultant once told me about a turning point in her career.

She'd just joined a new firm and quickly noticed tension with her project manager. Every meeting felt like a power struggle – she thought he didn't respect her expertise, and he thought she was defensive.

After a particularly heated discussion, she paused and decided to observe instead of reacting. The next day, she noticed something subtle – he interrupted *everyone*, not just her!

It wasn't personal – it was his way of thinking aloud.

That small realisation changed everything. Instead of taking offence, she began to ask questions before responding. Within weeks, their dynamic shifted from friction to flow.

Next-Level Skills

That's emotional intelligence in action – the moment understanding replaces assumption.

As Daniel Goleman, who popularised the concept of Emotional Intelligence, wrote:

"If your emotional abilities aren't in hand, if you don't have self-awareness, if you are not able to manage your distressing emotions, if you can't have empathy and effective relationships, then no matter how smart you are, you are not going to get very far."

Chapter 2: Emotional Intelligence

Why Emotional Intelligence Matters

In today's world, intelligence alone is no longer enough.

Technical mastery can get you into a job or profession – but emotional intelligence determines how far ahead and up you'll go.

Emotional Intelligence shapes how we manage stress, handle conflict, motivate others, and navigate the *'messy'* human side of work.

It's the skill behind all the "soft skills" that make-or-break careers.

Next-Level Skills

Here's why emotional intelligence matters so much:

Emotional Intelligence
Why It Matters!

1	**Improves communication and collaboration**
2	**Reduces stress and conflict**
3	**Strengthens leadership presence**
4	**Enhances resilience**
5	**Inspires loyalty**

Improves communication and collaboration

Emotional intelligence enables you to pick up on subtle cues such as tone, body language, and the energy behind words. This deeper understanding helps you communicate more clearly, listen actively, and address misunderstandings before they escalate. As a result, teamwork becomes smoother, and group problem-solving becomes more effective.

Reduces stress and conflict

When you respond to challenges with self-control and empathy rather than immediate reaction, situations are less likely to escalate into arguments or hostility. This ability to remain composed under pressure helps to create a calmer, more positive work environment where issues can be addressed constructively instead of turning into ongoing disputes.

Strengthens leadership presence

Leaders with high emotional intelligence are trusted because they combine warmth, approachability, and compassion with decisive action. They can motivate their teams, make tough decisions with sensitivity, and adapt their leadership style to different situations, which inspires confidence and respect from others.

Enhances resilience

Being attuned to your emotions means you can process setbacks and disappointments more effectively. Rather than getting stuck or overwhelmed, emotionally intelligent people can reflect on challenges, learn from them, and bounce back faster, maintaining motivation and optimism even when things don't go as planned.

Inspires loyalty

When team members feel genuinely understood, valued, and supported by their leaders and colleagues, they are more likely to remain committed and engaged. This sense of belonging and psychological safety fosters loyalty, reduces turnover, and encourages people to put in their best effort.

Chapter 2: Emotional Intelligence

A Harvard study found that emotional intelligence accounts for **nearly 90% of what sets high performers apart from peers with similar technical skills and IQ levels** (Goleman, 1998).

This finding has fundamentally reshaped how we understand workplace success and leadership effectiveness. Yet emotional intelligence remains widely misunderstood in professional contexts.

It's not about being "*emotional.*"

It's about being emotionally *literate* – knowing what's happening within yourself and others and managing it with wisdom and intentionality.

This distinction matters profoundly. Emotional literacy involves recognizing the subtle shifts in your own emotional landscape before they escalate into reactive behaviour.

It means accurately reading the unspoken signals in a room – the tension beneath polite agreement, the

Next-Level Skills

hesitation that signals doubt, the enthusiasm that indicates genuine buy-in.

Most critically, it requires the regulatory capacity to respond thoughtfully rather than react instinctively, even under pressure (Salovey & Mayer, 1990; Brackett, Rivers, & Salovey, 2011)

How do you move forward from understanding what emotional intelligence is to building it for real?

So, let's get right into some practical steps to practice and develop this skill.

Practical Ways to Build Emotional Intelligence

Emotional intelligence isn't a fixed trait you either possess or lack.

Emotional intelligence isn't hardwired.

It's a learnable capability you can cultivate through deliberate awareness, empathy, and consistent reflection.

How do I strengthen it in daily life?

Try these 6 practical ways to develop your emotional intelligence:

Next-Level Skills

Step 1: Name What You Feel

Most of us experience emotions faster than we can name them.

Start small – pause and ask,

> *"What am I feeling right now?"*

Not just "good" or "bad," but *curious, tense, hopeful, anxious, relieved, proud.*

(I know! There can be so many emotions at play.)

Labelling emotions accurately gives you control over them.

What you can name, you can navigate.

Step 2: Observe Before You Respond

When you feel triggered – by a comment, email, or tone – take a mental step back. Ask:

"What's really being said here?"

Emotionally intelligent people don't rush to react. They buy a moment of space between stimulus and response and decode their next steps from a level-headed mind.

That pause is the power.

Next-Level Skills

Step 3: Read the Room

Look beyond words.

Notice posture, tone, pace, and micro-expressions.

When someone says, "I'm fine," but their voice tightens – tune in.

Emotional Intelligence is often about what's *unsaid*.

The better you read emotional cues, the more effectively you'll navigate relationships.

Step 4: Practice Empathic Curiosity

Empathy isn't agreement – it's understanding.

When someone disagrees with you, replace judgment with curiosity. Ask,

"Help me understand what's important to you here?"

Empathic curiosity builds bridges faster than any argument can.

Next-Level Skills

Step 5: Regulate Before You Communicate

Before responding in heated moments, take one grounding breath.

Ask yourself:

What outcome do I want?

Will my next words move me closer or further from it?

Emotional regulation doesn't silence emotion – it channels it.

Chapter 2: Emotional Intelligence

Step 6: Lead with Emotional Transparency

Leaders who name emotions set the tone for psychological safety.

Saying below models honesty and calm.

"I'm feeling stretched but confident we'll get there,"

Transparency invites trust – and trust fuels performance.

"Emotional intelligence isn't about being nice all the time. It's about being real at the right time."

Let's look through the stories of people who've demonstrated emotional intelligence at best in the face of some of the unimaginable circumstances.

Next-Level Skills

Skill in Action: Real-World Examples

Jacinda Ardern's Empathetic Leadership in Crisis

When tragedy struck Christchurch in 2019, New Zealand's PM, Jacinda Ardern didn't hide behind policy briefings or distant rhetoric. Instead, she stood among mourners, her voice steady yet warm, offering words of compassion and unity. She wore a headscarf in solidarity with the Muslim community, a gesture that spoke louder than speeches.

Her leadership wasn't about emotional display but emotional tunning. She listened deeply, responded with humility, and humanised authority. The world took notice because empathy was not used as strategy — it was authenticity in motion. Her composure, rooted in emotional intelligence, turned crisis management into collective healing at national level.

Empathy is strength expressed with softness.

Satya Nadella's Culture of Empathy

Upon assuming Microsoft's leadership, Satya Nadella inherited an organization that excelled at innovation but struggled with internal cooperation. As explored in the Self-Awareness chapter earlier, he drew upon his own life experiences and diverse viewpoints to develop his leadership approach, championing the idea throughout Microsoft that empathy represents a strategic strength, not a vulnerability.

This philosophy became embedded in Microsoft's organizational culture. Team discussions shifted from fault-finding to inquisitiveness. Setbacks were reframed as learning opportunities rather than final judgments. Nadella consistently emphasized to his teams that behind every product and software feature lies a real person. By connecting empathetic leadership with business outcomes, he transformed Microsoft into not only a more effective organization but also a more compassionate one.

Empathy multiplies engagement.

Next-Level Skills

Michelle Obama's Emotional Honesty in Public Life

In her memoir *Becoming*, Michelle Obama revealed the moments of self-doubt that accompanied her public life – from juggling motherhood to enduring relentless scrutiny. Instead of crafting a perfect image, she shared an honest one: the fatigue, the small victories, and the ongoing negotiation between ambition and authenticity. That openness became a mirror for readers, helping them recognise their own emotions without shame.

Her approach redefined strength for women in leadership. By allowing vulnerability to coexist with confidence, she modelled how emotional intelligence involves both self-awareness and self-expression. Millions felt seen because she chose to be real.

Authenticity connects deeper than perfection.

Chapter 2: Emotional Intelligence

Tim Cook's Empathetic Approach at Apple

When Tim Cook succeeded Steve Jobs, expectations were immense. Instead of replicating Jobs' intensity, Cook led Apple with steadiness and empathy. He spent his early years listening – not only to engineers and designers but to everyday employees across departments. His quiet "*authority-built*" safety, encouraged creativity to flourish without fear.

Cook's emotional intelligence showed that humility and strength are not opposites. He prioritised inclusion, sustainability, and accessibility, making Apple a company where innovation and compassion coexisted. Through presence rather than performance, he proved that empathy sustains excellence long after charisma fades.

Quiet empathy sustains lasting impact.

Malala Yousafzai's Emotional Courage

At fifteen, Malala Yousafzai was attacked for advocating girls' education. Her recovery could have been a story of retreat, yet she turned pain into purpose. Rather than dwell in anger, she channelled empathy – even towards those who harmed her. That inner composure, the ability to feel deeply yet act wisely, embodied emotional intelligence at its highest form.

Malala used her story to build bridges across cultures, not walls of resentment. Her poise in public appearances radiates both conviction and compassion. She reminds the world that emotional intelligence is not just corporate currency – it's moral leadership in action.

Emotional balance turns adversity into advocacy.

Chapter 2: Emotional Intelligence

Weekly Reflection Exercise

Take 10 quiet minutes to reflect on these:

- *When did I last feel emotionally triggered, and how did I handle it?*
- *How attuned am I to the emotions of those around me?*
- *What's one recurring situation where my emotions tend to lead instead of guide?*
- *How can I practice empathy in my next conversation – especially with someone I find challenging?*

Reflection turns emotional moments into emotional growth.

Next-Level Skills

One Key Action Step This Week

Before your next difficult conversation, take one deep breath and set an intention:

"I want to understand before I react."

Then notice what changes — in tone, in energy, and in outcome.

That single shift can transform the entire conversation.

Chapter 2: Emotional Intelligence

Final Reflection

Emotional intelligence isn't about suppressing emotions – it's about *synchronising* them with your intentions.

It's the calm within chaos, the warmth behind strength, and the reason some people make others feel seen while others don't. It's what turns knowledge into connection, and leadership into influence.

As Maya Angelou beautifully said:

"People will forget what you said, people will forget what you did, but people will never forget how you made them feel."

When you master emotional intelligence, you don't just manage emotions –

You elevate every interaction you touch!

Next-Level Skills

Chapter Immediately

Emotional Intelligence

WHY IT MATTERS!

- ⭐ Improves communication and collaboration
- ⭐ Reduces stress and conflict
- ⭐ Strengthens leadership presence
- ⭐ Enhances resilience
- ⭐ Inspires loyalty

PRACTICAL WAYS TO BUILD THE SKILL

1. Name What You Feel
2. Observe Before You Respond
3. Read the Room
4. Practice Empathic Curiosity
5. Regulate Before You Communicate
6. Lead with Emotional Transparency

Chapter 2: Emotional Intelligence

Take It Further ...

- *How do you typically react when emotions run high and what patterns do you notice?*

- *In what ways can empathy improve your relationships at work and at home?*

- *How can emotional intelligence help you navigate difficult feedback or conflict?*

- *What daily habits can help you stay emotionally grounded?*

- *How do you ensure you're listening to understand, not just to reply?*

- *What's one emotion you often suppress and what might it be teaching you?*

- *How can emotional intelligence help you lead with both strength and compassion?*

Next-Level Skills

- *How do you recover after an emotionally charged situation, and what strategies can help you regain balance quickly?*

- *In what ways can you model emotionally intelligent behaviour to inspire those around you?*

- *How do you recognise when your emotions are influencing your decisions, and what steps do you take to ensure clarity?*

- *What role does self-reflection play in building your emotional intelligence over time?*

Chapter 3: Active Listening

"The Hidden Power Behind Every Great Conversation"

Next-Level Skills

Building on *Emotional Intelligence*, active listening turns empathy into action.

It's the bridge between *understanding emotions* and *responding with intention*. True listening isn't passive – it's presence in motion.

In an age where distractions are constant and attention is currency, active listening has become one of the rarest – and most powerful – professional skills.

Chapter 3: Active Listening

"Hearing Isn't the Same as Listening"

When a senior HR manager at a global tech firm noticed tension between two high-performing team leads, she scheduled a mediation session.

She opened the meeting by saying, "I'm not here to decide who's right – I just want to understand what's happening."

Then she did something most leaders forget to do – she listened without interrupting.

Each person spoke for five minutes while the other could only take notes.

By the end, both were surprised. Neither had truly *heard* the other before. They'd been waiting to respond, not to understand.

That meeting didn't just resolve the conflict – it rebuilt trust.

Next-Level Skills

Listening didn't cost her anything.

But it changed everything.

"Most people do not listen with the intent to understand. They listen with the intent to reply."
– Stephen R. Covey

Chapter 3: Active Listening

Why Active Listening Matters

Active listening is more than hearing words – it's tuning into *meaning, tone, and emotion.*

It's the skill that transforms conversations from transactions into connections.

When we truly listen, we create space for others to be fully seen and understood. This means setting aside our own agenda, resisting the urge to interrupt with solutions, and instead leaning into the speaker's experience with genuine curiosity.

It involves reading between the lines – noticing what's left unsaid, picking up on subtle shifts in energy, and recognizing the feelings beneath the facts.

Active listeners don't just wait for their turn to speak, they engage with questions that deepen understanding and reflect back what they've heard to ensure alignment. This level of attention signals respect and builds trust in ways that polished responses never could.

Next-Level Skills

Here's why listening actively is essential:

Active Listening
Why It Matters!

1	Builds trust and rapport
2	Reduces misunderstandings
3	Enhances influence
4	Improves problem-solving
5	Boosts leadership presence

Builds trust and rapport

When people feel genuinely listened to, they sense that their opinions truly matter. This validation helps set up trust and strengthen connections, making individuals feel respected and valued within the group or organisation.

Reduces misunderstandings

Taking the time to clarify the meaning behind what's being said significantly lowers the risk of miscommunication. By actively listening and asking thoughtful questions, you can address potential confusion before it turns into unnecessary conflict.

Enhances influence

The act of listening closely shows that you care about others' perspectives. As a result, when you do speak, your words carry greater weight and credibility because people know you've taken their input into account.

Next-Level Skills

Improves problem-solving

Active listening allows you to dig deeper and uncover the real issues beneath the surface. By understanding everyone's concerns and viewpoints, you can identify better solutions that address the root cause of challenges.

Boosts leadership presence

Exceptional leaders make each person feel as if they're the only one in the room. By giving others your undivided attention, you demonstrate respect and empathy, which inspires loyalty and encourages honest communication throughout your team.

In teams, listening acts like oil in a machine – invisible but essential for smooth motion.

And just like any other skill, it can be trained, strengthened, and mastered.

Chapter 3: Active Listening

Practical Ways to Build Active Listening

Active listening isn't about staying silent – it's about being *strategically attentive.*

The distinction is crucial: passive silence can feel distant or disengaging, while active listening is a dynamic practice that requires full presence and intentional engagement.

It means seeing body language, keeping proper eye contact, and using verbal cues to encourage the speaker to continue.

Developing this capacity requires moving beyond theory into deliberate practice. While the concept of active listening may seem intuitive, implementing it consistently demands specific techniques and sustained effort.

Here are six practical steps to develop it in your daily interactions.

Next-Level Skills

Step 1: Be Fully Present

Before every important conversation, put away distractions.

Silence notifications, close your laptop, and give your full attention.

Presence is the first signal of respect and hence, the foundation of listening.

Chapter 3: Active Listening

Step 2: Listen to Understand, Not to Reply

As Stephen Covey said, most people listen to respond.

Flip that mindset: focus on what the other person *means*, not just what they *say*.

Ask yourself silently:

"What are they really trying to express?"

Next-Level Skills

Step 3: Reflect and Paraphrase

After the speaker finishes, summarise in your own words:

"So, what I'm hearing is..."

This small phrase does wonders. It shows understanding, checks accuracy, and builds connection.

Step 4: Read the Unsaid

True listening goes beyond ears – it involves eyes and empathy.

Notice tone, pace, posture, and micro-expressions.

When words say, "*I'm fine,*" but eyes say otherwise, listen with curiosity, not correction.

Next-Level Skills

Step 5: Ask Clarifying Questions

Good listeners ask questions that deepen understanding, not control it. Try:

"Can you tell me more about that?"

or

"What matters most to you here?"

Questions like these open doors to insight – and often defuse tension.

Step 6: Respond with Empathy and Intention

Once you've understood, respond with care. Instead of advice, start with validation:

"I can see why that felt frustrating." or *"That sounds really important to you."*

When people feel heard, they open up to influence.

"When someone really hears you without passing judgment... it feels damn good."
– Carl Rogers

Let's look through the stories of people who've set great examples of active listening and inspired us to become better listeners.

Skill in Action: Real-World Examples

Nelson Mandela's Deep Listening Leadership

When Nelson Mandela emerged from 27 years in prison, his instinct wasn't to speak first – it was to listen. During the delicate negotiations that ended apartheid, he invited adversaries into dialogue and treated even the most hostile voices with respect. He often leaned back, hands clasped, eyes focused, allowing silence to fill the room until others had fully spoken.

Mandela's listening became his most powerful political tool. He made people feel heard – not agreed with but acknowledged. That simple act diffused tension, restored dignity, and paved the way for reconciliation. His leadership reminds us that listening is an instrument of peace.

True listening disarms resistance.

Indra Nooyi's "Listen to Understand" Practice

When Indra Nooyi became CEO of PepsiCo, she was determined to stay grounded despite leading a global empire. She often spent time in the field – visiting factories, stores, and community centres – speaking directly with employees and customers. Instead of delivering speeches, she asked open questions and listened intently to their experiences. "You can't lead from spreadsheets," she once said. "You lead from conversations."

This practice gave her insights that data never could – about morale, customer expectations, and social impact. By truly listening, Nooyi built a company culture where people felt valued, not managed. Her leadership showed that growth comes from the ears, not just the boardroom.

Listening expands vision beyond data.

Next-Level Skills

Barack Obama's Reflective Conversations

During his presidency, Barack Obama was often praised for his calm demeanour in high-pressure situations. One of his trademarks was active listening. In meetings, he would rephrase what others said before responding, ensuring understanding and validation. This small gesture had a profound effect – it encouraged candour, even among dissenting voices.

Obama believed leadership meant making space for truth. His listening didn't just extract information. It built trust. Whether addressing global leaders or town-hall audiences, his presence conveyed one message: every voice matters. His legacy reminds us that listening is not about waiting to reply but about choosing to understand.

Listening is respect in action.

Mary Barra's Town Halls at General Motors

When General Motors faced its 2014 recall crisis, CEO Mary Barra chose transparency over defensiveness. She organised open town halls where employees could voice concerns directly – even critical ones. She stood on stage, took every question, and answered with honesty. By listening publicly and without judgment, she modelled accountability from the top.

The impact rippled across the company. Employees felt empowered to speak up about safety issues rather than conceal them. Barra's leadership proved that deep listening restores credibility faster than any PR campaign. It turns vulnerability into strength and scepticism into trust.

Listening restores trust faster than statements.

Next-Level Skills

The Dalai Lama's Mindful Conversations

When the Dalai Lama meets someone, he often greets them with a laugh – then listens quietly, his attention unwavering. His mindful pauses during dialogue aren't awkward silences. They're spaces of his full presence. He once said, "When you talk, you are only repeating what you already know. When you listen, you may learn something new." That approach turns every encounter into an exchange of insight, not just information.

His listening carries spiritual depth – a reminder that attention itself is an act of kindness. Whether addressing global audiences or individuals seeking guidance, his presence communicates care beyond words. Through mindful listening, he shows that peace begins in conversation, not decree.

Silence is the first act of listening.

Chapter 3: Active Listening

Weekly Reflection Exercise

Take 10 quiet minutes to reflect on these:

How often do I listen to reply versus to understand?

Who in my life do I interrupt most and why?

When was the last time someone made me feel truly heard?

How can I create that same experience for someone else this week?

Next-Level Skills

One Key Action Step This Week

In your next conversation – personal or professional – pause before responding.

Count to three silently, then reflect back one key point you heard.

You'll notice the quality of the conversation change instantly.

Chapter 3: Active Listening

Final Reflection

Active listening is the ultimate act of empathy.

It slows the rush of reaction and creates space for understanding.

It's what turns conversations into connection and connection into trust.

As Ernest Hemingway once said:

"When people talk, listen completely. Most people never listen."

In a world that's louder than ever, be the one who listens deeply.

That's how influence begins – quietly.

Next-Level Skills

Chapter Immediately

Active Listening

WHY IT MATTERS!

- ★ Builds trust and rapport
- ★ Reduces misunderstandings
- ★ Enhances influence
- ★ Improves problem-solving
- ★ Boosts leadership presence

PRACTICAL WAYS TO BUILD THE SKILL

1. Be Fully Present

2. Listen to Understand, Not to Reply

3. Reflect and Paraphrase

4. Read the Unsaid

5. Ask Clarifying Questions

6. Respond with Empathy and Intention

Chapter 3: Active Listening

Take It Further ...

- *How do you typically show someone that you're listening?*

- *What are your biggest distractions during conversations, and how can you minimise them?*

- *How does active listening help in conflict resolution?*

- *Who in your life deserves more of your full attention right now?*

- *How can reflective listening improve your leadership impact?*

- *What's one relationship that could transform if you simply listened better?*

- *How can you model active listening in your team or family?*

Next-Level Skills

- *What is one habit you can adopt to remind yourself to listen before reacting in conversations?*

- *How does your body language communicate that you are truly present with someone?*

- *How might your relationships change if you made a conscious effort to listen for what's not being said, as well as what is?*

Part II – The Adaptive Mindset: Thriving in Change

Self-awareness gives us understanding.
Emotional intelligence gives us balance.
Active listening gives us connection.

Together, they build a centred, grounded self – one capable of leading with clarity and empathy.

But awareness alone isn't enough.
The world keeps changing – faster, louder, and more unpredictably than ever.

To stay effective, we need to evolve from *knowing ourselves* to *adapting ourselves*.

That's where the next stage begins.

Next-Level Skills

Part II – *The Adaptive Mindset: Thriving in Change* – is about turning insight into movement.

It's about staying flexible without losing focus, seeing strategically without losing simplicity, and communicating with clarity even when everything around us feels uncertain.

Because growth isn't about staying still.

It's about learning to move – wisely, intentionally, and with purpose – no matter what changes around you.

PART II
The Adaptive Mindset: Thriving in Change

04   **Adaptability**
The Art of Staying Steady When Everything Changes

05   **Strategic Thinking**
Seeing the Forest and the Trees

06   **Clear Communication**
Turning Vision into Understanding

"Flexibility is the modern superpower"

Next-Level Skills

Chapter 4: Adaptability

"The Art of Staying Steady When Everything Changes"

Next-Level Skills

Building on *Active Listening*, adaptability takes what you hear, learn, and feel – and turns it into *fluid action*.

It's your ability to stay grounded when the ground beneath you, shifts.

In a world where change is no longer an event but a constant, adaptability has become one of the most valuable leadership and life skills.

Those who resist change get left behind.

Those who adapt – evolve.

Chapter 4: Adaptability

"The Pivot Point"

When the pandemic first hit, an event manager in Sydney saw her entire business vanish overnight.

Her calendar, once packed with corporate bookings, was suddenly blank.

After a week of shock and silence, she made a bold decision – instead of waiting for normal to return, she created her own version of it.

She started running virtual events, helping clients shift to online experiences. Within months, her business wasn't just surviving – it was growing faster than before.

Her adaptability didn't erase the challenge.

It redefined it.

Next-Level Skills

"It is not the strongest of the species that survive, nor the most intelligent, but the one most responsive to change."
– Charles Darwin

Chapter 4: Adaptability

Why Adaptability Matters

Adaptability isn't about having all the answers – it's about staying flexible enough to find them.

It's the skill that transforms uncertainty into opportunity.

In a world where change arrives faster than we can predict it, rigid thinking becomes a liability. Adaptable leaders don't cling to outdated playbooks or insist on plans simply because they were made. Instead, they read the shifting landscape with clear eyes, adjust their approach when evidence demands it, and embrace the discomfort that comes with pivoting.

This flexibility isn't weakness or indecision – it's intelligent responsiveness.

It means holding your strategies lightly while gripping your values firmly, recognizing that the path to your goals may look nothing like you originally imagined.

Next-Level Skills

Here's why adaptability matters:

Adaptability
Why It Matters!

1	**Drives innovation**
2	**Reduces stress**
3	**Improves problem-solving**
4	**Builds resilience**
5	**Elevates leadership**

Drives innovation

When you let go the mindset of "how it's always been," you open yourself up to new possibilities and fresh ideas. This openness allows you to spot trends, experiment with novel approaches, and implement creative solutions that others may overlook. Adaptable people are often the first to discover better ways of doing things, driving progress not just for themselves, but for their teams and organisations as well.

Reduces stress

Accepting change as a natural part of life helps shift your mindset from resistance to acceptance. Instead of feeling overwhelmed by uncertainty, you learn to ride the waves of change with greater ease. This acceptance fosters a sense of calm and control, making challenges feel more manageable and reducing the emotional toll that comes with ambiguity and unexpected disruptions.

Next-Level Skills

Improves problem-solving

Adaptable individuals approach obstacles with a flexible mindset, considering multiple pathways rather than getting stuck on one solution. This ability to think in options rather than limitations allows for more effective and creative problem-solving. When faced with adversity, you can pivot quickly, try different approaches, and ultimately find solutions that may not have been immediately obvious.

Builds resilience

As you become more comfortable with change, transitions start to feel less chaotic and more like part of a natural evolution. Each challenge you overcome strengthens your capacity to recover quickly and thrive in new circumstances. Adaptability helps you bounce back from setbacks and maintain momentum, even when the road ahead is unknown or uncertain.

Chapter 4: Adaptability

Elevates leadership

Leaders who demonstrate adaptability inspire confidence in others, especially during times of uncertainty. By remaining calm, open to feedback, and willing to adjust plans as needed, adaptable leaders set a positive example for their teams. This behaviour fosters trust and motivates others to embrace change, knowing they are guided by someone who can navigate complex situations with clarity and composure.

As Carol Dweck, author of *Mindset*, noted:

"Becoming is better than being."

Adaptability is the skill of *becoming* – of continuously learning, experimenting, and staying curious even when plans fall apart.

Next-Level Skills

Practical Ways to Build Adaptability

Adaptability grows through awareness, experimentation, and reframing. These three pillars work in concert to build genuine flexibility.

Awareness means recognizing your default patterns — the mental models and assumptions that guide your responses to change.

Experimentation involves deliberately stepping outside your comfort zone, testing new approaches and treating each attempt, however small, as data rather than destiny.

Reframing is perhaps the most powerful lever: it's the ability to look at the same situation through a different lens and extract new meaning.

Combining these practices, adaptability, a tangible skill, can be developed systematically. Here are six steps to strengthen it in daily life.

Chapter 4: Adaptability

Step 1: Reframe Uncertainty as Information

Instead of seeing change as chaos, view it as data. Ask:

"What is this situation teaching me?"

Every disruption carries insight – only if you're willing to look for it.

Next-Level Skills

Step 2: Practice Micro-Flexibility

Adaptability doesn't always mean huge pivots.

It starts small – a changed routine, a new idea, a different conversation approach.

Small flexes build big resilience.

Step 3: Stay Curious, Not Certain

Certainty closes doors. Curiosity opens them.

When something unexpected happens, ask:

"What else could be true here?"

Curiosity turns resistance into discovery.

Next-Level Skills

Step 4: Learn Fast, Fail Smart

Adaptable people don't fear mistakes – they extract lessons.

Instead of asking,

"Why did this fail?"

they ask,

"What did this teach me?"

That subtle shift changes everything.

Step 5: Regulate Emotion Before Reaction

Adaptability isn't just mental – it's emotional.

When change hits, pause before reacting.

Breathe.

Name what you feel.

Then respond with perspective, not panic.

Next-Level Skills

Step 6: Embrace Continuous Reinvention

Schedule time to review your habits, routines, and assumptions. Ask:

"What used to work that no longer serves me?"

Growth requires pruning – letting go of old systems to make room for new strength.

"Inflexibility is the worst form of weakness."
– Charles de Gaulle

Chapter 4: Adaptability

Skill in Action: Real-World Examples

Netflix's Reinvention

In the early 2000s, Netflix was a mail-order DVD rental company. The model worked well – until technology started moving faster than postage. Rather than clinging to its success, co-founder Reed Hastings began preparing for obsolescence. He famously said, "We're not in the DVD business. We're in the entertainment business." That mental shift – redefining the problem – allowed Netflix to pivot towards streaming long before it became mainstream.

The transition required dismantling their existing profitable business and learning entirely new skills. Netflix not only survived the digital revolution but shaped it – proof that foresight is the deepest form of flexibility.

True adaptability means changing before you have to.

Toyota's Continuous Improvement Mindset (Kaizen)

In the aftermath of World War II, Japan's economy was in ruins. Toyota, then a small car manufacturer, faced shortages, inefficiencies, and intense competition. Instead of resisting change, the company embraced it – developing the now-famous *Kaizen* philosophy of continuous improvement. Every worker, from executives to factory line operators, was empowered to find and fix inefficiencies daily.

This culture of small, steady adaptation transformed Toyota into a global benchmark for resilience and quality. More importantly, it showed that adaptability isn't a reaction to crisis but a daily discipline. When every challenge is seen as an opportunity to gain experience, change becomes the norm, not the exception.

Adaptability is built one improvement at a time.

Chapter 4: Adaptability

J.K. Rowling's Reinvention Through Rejection

Before *Harry Potter* became a global phenomenon, J.K. Rowling faced twelve rejections from publishers. As a single mother living on welfare, she rewrote and reimagined her manuscript multiple times, adapting her story and style based on feedback and failure. Each rejection wasn't a wall – it was a rewrite.

When the series finally succeeded, Rowling's story became a modern parable for resilience and reinvention. She often says that "rock bottom became the solid foundation" on which she rebuilt her life. Adaptability, for her, wasn't just about craft – it was about self-transformation through persistence.

Adaptability grows in the space between failure and persistence.

Next-Level Skills

NASA's Apollo 13: "Failure Is Not an Option"

In 1970, an oxygen tank explosion crippled Apollo 13's spacecraft mid-mission. The team at NASA's Mission Control faced an impossible scenario: bring the astronauts home safely with limited power, oxygen, and time. They re-engineered solutions on the fly, using only materials available aboard the craft – including duct tape. Every decision required rapid adaptation under life-or-death pressure.

Their success wasn't luck but mindset. Years of cultivating creative problem-solving and calm under uncertainty paid off when it mattered most. The Apollo 13 mission became a timeless symbol of adaptability: the ability to adjust, improvise, and succeed when plans collapse.

Adaptability turns crisis into creativity.

Chapter 4: Adaptability

Serena Williams: Reinventing Herself Across Eras

Few athletes have reinvented themselves as completely – and as often – as Serena Williams. Over two decades, she adjusted her playing style, fitness routines, and mental approach to stay at the top of her sport. After injuries and motherhood, she redefined her training to align with her evolving body and priorities.

Her adaptability wasn't just physical – it was emotional. She learned when to be fierce, when to be patient, and when to rest. In a sport defined by change, Serena's ability to evolve without losing her essence illustrates that adaptability is not about compromise – it's about conscious reinvention.

Adaptability is staying true to yourself while evolving beyond your limits.

Next-Level Skills

Weekly Reflection Exercise

Take 10 quiet minutes to reflect on these:

How do I typically respond to unexpected changes?

What's one recent disruption that taught me something valuable?

Where in my life am I resisting flexibility – and why?

How can I cultivate curiosity instead of control in the week ahead?

Chapter 4: Adaptability

One Key Action Step This Week

Next time something doesn't go as planned, pause and say to yourself:

"This is data, not disaster."

Then note what new possibilities appear once you release resistance.

Next-Level Skills

Final Reflection

Adaptability is courage in motion.

It's what allows you to move forward when certainty disappears – and to trust that growth often hides behind disruption.

As Bruce Lee famously said:

"Be water, my friend."

The most adaptable leaders and learners don't just survive change – they shape it.

Chapter Immediately

Adaptability

WHY IT MATTERS!

- ⭐ Drives innovation
- ⭐ Reduces stress
- ⭐ Improves problem-solving
- ⭐ Builds resilience
- ⭐ Elevates leadership

PRACTICAL WAYS TO BUILD THE SKILL

1. Reframe Uncertainty as Information

2. Practice Micro-Flexibility

3. Stay Curious, Not Certain

4. Learn Fast, Fail Smart

5. Regulate Emotion Before Reaction

6. Embrace Continuous Reinvention

Next-Level Skills

Take It Further ...

- *How do you usually react when plans fall apart?*

- *In what ways can reframing uncertainty help you stay calm under pressure?*

- *How can small, daily flexibility make you more resilient to bigger shifts?*

- *What's one outdated habit or assumption you need to release this month?*

- *How does emotional regulation support adaptability?*

- *Who do you know that models adaptability well – and what can you learn from them?*

- *How can you cultivate a culture of adaptability in your team or workplace?*

Chapter 4: Adaptability

- *How do you encourage others to embrace change rather than resist it?*

- *What strategies help you maintain focus and motivation during uncertain times?*

- *How can you use feedback from unexpected outcomes to improve future adaptability?*

Next-Level Skills

Chapter 5: Strategic Thinking

"Seeing the Forest and the Trees"

Next-Level Skills

Building on *Adaptability*, strategic thinking is how you channel flexibility into foresight.

If adaptability helps you pivot, strategic thinking helps you *predict where to pivot next*.

It's the ability to zoom out from the chaos of daily tasks, spot emerging patterns, and make decisions today that serve tomorrow.

In a world obsessed with speed, the most valuable leaders aren't just fast — they're *forward-thinking*.

Chapter 5: Strategic Thinking

"From Busy to Brilliant"

A project director at a major infrastructure firm once confessed that he was exhausted – not from lack of work ethic, but from being caught in constant urgency.

Every day was a race: emails, deadlines, approvals, meetings.

One day, his mentor asked him a simple question:

"Are you moving things forward or just keeping them moving?"

That stopped him cold.

He realised he was managing activity, not advancing strategy.

The next week, he blocked out one hour every Friday titled *'Thinking Time.'*

No emails. No meetings. Just space to look at the bigger picture.

Within months, he noticed a shift: his decisions got sharper, his team became more initiative-taking, and his stress levels dropped.

That's the difference between being reactive and being strategic.

"The essence of strategy is choosing what not to do."

– Michael Porter

Chapter 5: Strategic Thinking

Why Strategic Thinking Matters

Strategic thinking isn't about having all the answers – it's about asking better questions.

It allows you to connect dots others don't even see yet.

While others focus on immediate problems, strategic thinkers zoom out to understand the larger patterns at play. They don't just react to what's in front of them – they anticipate what's around the corner.

This means distinguishing between what's urgent and what's important, recognizing that today's small decisions can create tomorrow's big outcomes.

Strategic thinkers hold multiple perspectives simultaneously, weighing trade-offs and second-order consequences before committing to action. They see systems rather than silos, understanding how different elements interact and influence each other over time. When you develop strategic thinking, you stop being surprised by change – you start shaping it.

Next-Level Skills

Here's why thinking strategically is essential:

Strategic Thinking
Why It Matters!

1	**Creates direction amid uncertainty**
2	**Turns chaos into clarity**
3	**Builds long-term influence**
4	**Drives innovation**
5	**Prevents burnout**

Creates direction amid uncertainty

When everything feels up in the air, strategic thinking helps you set a clear destination. Rather than simply reacting to whatever comes your way, you consciously define where you want to go, not just how to get there. This clarity allows you and your team to stay focused, even when circumstances change or information is incomplete.

Turns chaos into clarity

With competing priorities and constant distractions, it's easy to get lost in the noise. Strategic thinking enables you to cut through the confusion by identifying what truly matters. You learn to filter out what's irrelevant, focus your energy on high-impact areas, and create order out of disorder, giving your efforts greater purpose and direction.

Builds long-term influence

People naturally look to those who can see beyond the immediate situation. When you consistently think ahead, anticipate challenges, and plan for the future, others begin to trust your judgement and perspective. This foresight helps you earn respect and become a guiding force within your team or organisation over the long haul.

Drives innovation

Strategic thinkers don't just solve existing problems. They actively look for new opportunities and unexplored paths. By questioning assumptions and imagining different possibilities, you can spark creative solutions and encourage your team to experiment. This mindset leads to fresh ideas and keeps your approach dynamic and forward-thinking.

Prevents burnout

When you approach your work strategically, you prioritise tasks that align with your biggest goals and delegate or drop low-value activities. This means you're not just working harder but working smarter. Over time, this reduces unnecessary stress, helps you maintain balance, and ensures you're making meaningful progress without sacrificing your health.

Chapter 5: Strategic Thinking

As Simon Sinek beautifully puts it:

"Leadership is not about being in charge. It's about taking care of those in your charge – and thinking ahead for them."

Next-Level Skills

Practical Ways to Build Strategic Thinking

Strategic thinking is like a muscle — it strengthens through reflection, curiosity, and disciplined focus.

The difference between tactical and strategic thinking lies not in complexity but in perspective — the ability to step back from the day-to-day rush and examine the bigger picture with intention.

Reflection creates space to extract lessons from experience. Curiosity drives you to explore beyond your immediate domain, seeking diverse inputs that spark new connections. Disciplined focus ensures you're not just thinking broadly but thinking productively, channelling your mental energy towards questions that truly matter.

When practiced consistently, these habits rewire how you approach problems, transforming reactive decision-making into proactive vision-building.
Here are practical ways to start thinking strategically.

Step 1: Ask "What's the Bigger Picture?"

Before reacting to a task or decision, pause and ask:

"How does this fit into the larger goal?"

This single question shifts your mindset from *doer* to *designer*.

Step 2: Think in Horizons

Divide your thinking into three levels:

Now – What needs immediate attention?

Next – What's coming in 3–6 months?

Beyond – What will matter in 1–3 years?

Strategic thinkers plan across time, not just tasks.

Step 3: Connect the Dots

Strategy often emerges from patterns.

Look for trends, repeated challenges, and recurring opportunities. Ask:

"What's the link between these events?"

The answers you find in the patterns reveal the path forward.

Next-Level Skills

Step 4: Scenario-Map Your Decisions

Before deciding, imagine at least two alternate futures. Ask:

"If I do X, what could happen short-term – and long-term?"

This foresight builds flexibility and resilience.

Step 5: Create Thinking Space

You can't think strategically if your calendar never breathes.

Schedule uninterrupted "thinking blocks."

Reflection time is not a luxury – it's a strategy in itself.

Next-Level Skills

Step 6: Simplify to Amplify

Complex problems tempt complex solutions. Strategic thinkers cut through noise by asking:

"What's the simplest action that will create the biggest impact?"

"In the midst of chaos, there is also opportunity."

– Sun Tzu

Chapter 5: Strategic Thinking

Skill in Action: Real-World Examples

Steve Jobs and the Art of Connecting the Dots

When Steve Jobs addressed Stanford graduates in 2005, he spoke about "connecting the dots" – the ability to trust that your diverse experiences will one day form a pattern. As a young man, Jobs dropped out of college but remained curious. Years later, that curiosity became a cornerstone of Apple's design philosophy – the obsession with typography and simplicity that defined the brand.

Jobs' genius was in pattern recognition. He saw what others didn't – the intersection of technology, design, and emotion. Strategic thinking, in his world, was equal parts vision and intuition. He showed that long-term clarity often comes from short-term curiosity.

Strategy begins with seeing connections where others see chaos.

Amazon's Long-Game Philosophy under Jeff Bezos

When Jeff Bezos founded Amazon, he famously told investors that profits would come later. While others chased quarterly gains, he chased customer trust. His guiding principle – "Start with the customer and work backwards" – became the north star for every product decision, from Kindle to Prime. Bezos' patience and foresight allowed Amazon to dominate industries by aligning every move to a clear long-term vision.

Strategic thinking, for Bezos, wasn't about predicting the future but preparing for it. He built structures and systems that thrived in uncertainty. While critics focused on short-term losses, Bezos remained investing in momentum. That ability to delay gratification and plan in decades, not quarters, transformed retail forever.

Strategic thinkers sacrifice immediacy for impact.

Chapter 5: Strategic Thinking

Elon Musk's Multi-Planet Vision

Elon Musk often describes himself as "an engineer with a deadline for the future." When he founded SpaceX, his goal wasn't merely to launch rockets – it was to make humanity multiplanetary. Critics called it impossible. Yet Musk's ability to link ambition with technical precision – to see the next 50 years instead of the next five – is the essence of strategic thinking.

At SpaceX and Tesla, he broke complex goals into solvable problems, using first-principles reasoning rather than industry assumptions. His vision of reusable rockets wasn't just a technical leap. It was a mindset shift – questioning limits, not accepting them. His boldness shows that true strategic thinkers look where others refuse to.

Strategic vision lives at the intersection of imagination and discipline.

Next-Level Skills

Sheryl Sandberg and Building Resilience into Strategy

When Sheryl Sandberg joined Facebook as COO, the company was growing rapidly but lacked operational structure. She introduced systems that allowed the business to scale without losing its agility. Her approach combined analytical clarity with empathy — strategy rooted in understanding both people and process.

Later, when faced with personal tragedy, Sandberg's public reflections presented in her book, *Option B,* demonstrated that strategic thinking applies beyond business — it's how we navigate loss, rebuild structure, and plan our way back to strength. Her story illustrates that strategy is not only corporate but deeply human: the art of finding forward motion amid uncertainty.

Resilience is strategy under pressure.

Chapter 5: Strategic Thinking

Winston Churchill's Vision in Wartime

During World War II, Winston Churchill's strategic genius lay not in tactics but in timing and morale. Facing overwhelming odds, he refused to surrender Britain's spirit. His speeches were not only political but psychological strategies – shaping public emotion to sustain national resilience. Behind the rhetoric was foresight: Churchill knew that survival required belief as much as arms.

His decisions often carried long-term consequences that only he seemed to see at the time. By balancing immediate defence with postwar vision, he ensured that Britain didn't just endure – it emerged ready to rebuild. Churchill's leadership reminds us that strategy is both a plan and a story people choose to believe in.

Strategy is vision turned into collective courage.

Next-Level Skills

Weekly Reflection Exercise

Take 10 quiet minutes to reflect on these:

Do I spend more time reacting or thinking ahead?

What patterns have I noticed recently that could hint at bigger shifts?

How much time each week do I dedicate to reflection or strategic review?

What's one current challenge I can reframe into a long-term opportunity?

Chapter 5: Strategic Thinking

One Key Action Step This Week

Block one hour on your calendar labelled *"Strategic Thinking."*

No emails. No tasks. Just space to zoom out and ask:

"Am I working on the right things – or just busy with things?"

That single hour can realign an entire quarter.

Next-Level Skills

Final Reflection

Strategic thinking is less about predicting the future and more about preparing for multiple futures.

It's what separates reaction from readiness – and activity from impact.

As Peter Drucker said:

"The best way to predict the future is to create it."

When you master strategic thinking, you stop chasing change – and start shaping it.

Chapter 5: Strategic Thinking

Chapter Immediately

Strategic Thinking

WHY IT MATTERS!

- ⭐ Creates direction amid uncertainty
- ⭐ Turns chaos into clarity
- ⭐ Builds long-term influence
- ⭐ Drives innovation
- ⭐ Prevents burnout

PRACTICAL WAYS TO BUILD THE SKILL

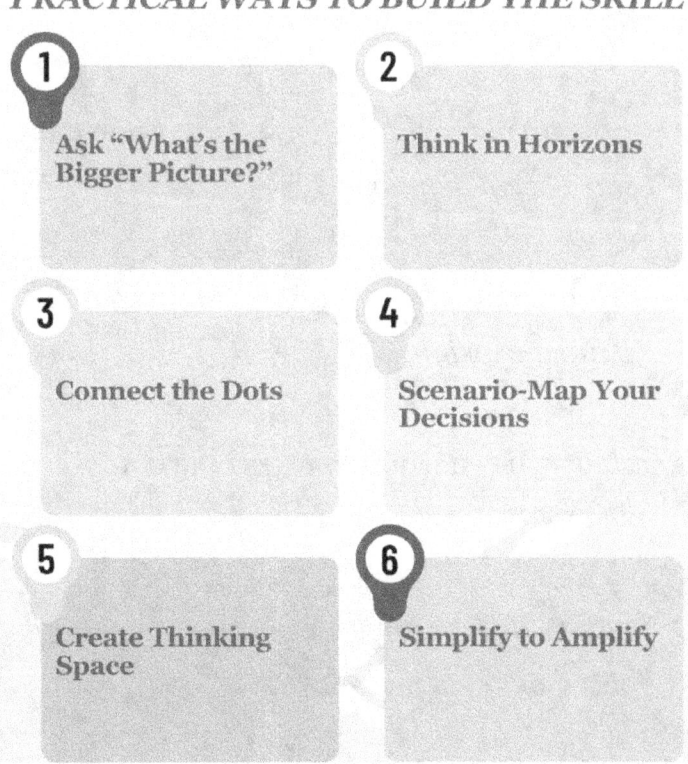

1. Ask "What's the Bigger Picture?"
2. Think in Horizons
3. Connect the Dots
4. Scenario-Map Your Decisions
5. Create Thinking Space
6. Simplify to Amplify

Next-Level Skills

Take It Further ...

- *What systems or routines help you zoom out and see the bigger picture?*

- *How can you apply strategic thinking to personal goals as well as professional ones?*

- *Who on your team naturally thinks strategically – and how can you learn from them?*

- *How do you balance long-term vision with short-term demands?*

- *What assumptions might be limiting your strategic insight?*

- *How can reflection time become a non-negotiable part of your week?*

- *What's one strategic opportunity you might be overlooking right now?*

Chapter 5: Strategic Thinking

- *How do external trends or shifts in your industry affect your strategic priorities?*

- *What feedback have you received recently that could spark a strategic rethink?*

- *Where could collaboration with another team or department unlock new strategic possibilities?*

Next-Level Skills

Chapter 6: Clear Communication

"Turning Vision into Understanding"

Next-Level Skills

Building on *Strategic Thinking*, clear communication is how you turn insight into influence.

It's one thing to see the bigger picture – it's another to express it in a way others can rally behind.

Great strategies fail not because they're weak, but because they're unclear.

Teams don't resist change – they resist *confusion*.

Clarity transforms ideas into action.

It bridges the gap between what you *mean* and what others *receive*.

In a noisy world full of competing messages, clarity is leadership.

"If you can't explain it simply, you don't understand it well enough."
– Albert Einstein

Chapter 6: Clear Communication

"Lost in Translation"

A regional manager at a logistics company once gave his team what he thought was a simple instruction:

"Let's prioritise customer satisfaction this quarter."

Three months later, he was frustrated – everyone had interpreted it differently.

One team extended delivery times to improve accuracy, another spent more on refunds, and another launched a new feedback form.

None of it aligned.

He realised that while his *intent* was clear in his head, his *message* wasn't clear in their minds.

The problem wasn't effort – it was *ambiguity*.

Next-Level Skills

"The single biggest problem in communication is the illusion that it has taken place."

– George Bernard Shaw

Chapter 6: Clear Communication

Why Clear Communication Matters

Clarity isn't about using fancy words – it's about removing the fog.

When you communicate clearly, people not only understand you – they trust you.

In a world drowning in information, clarity cuts through like a lighthouse beam. It's the difference between messages that get ignored and ideas that inspire action.

Clear communicators don't hide behind jargon, corporate speak, or unnecessary complexity. They distil their thoughts to their essence, choosing simple words over impressive ones, short sentences over meandering paragraphs.

When people grasp your message immediately, without having to decode or guess, they feel confident engaging with it. That confidence builds trust, because clarity signals honesty and competence.

Next-Level Skills

Here's why clarity in communication matters:

Clear Communication
Why It Matters!

1	Saves time and reduces rework
2	Strengthens credibility
3	Improves relationships
4	Enhances decision-making
5	Drives accountability

Saves time and reduces rework

When your message is clear, misunderstandings are minimised, allowing teams to work more efficiently. This means projects are completed faster, and there's less need to revisit or fix mistakes caused by miscommunication. Ultimately, clarity streamlines processes and frees up time for important tasks.

Strengthens credibility

People are more likely to respect and trust leaders who speak with precision and intention. Consistently clear communication demonstrates expertise and reliability, making it easier for others to have confidence in your decisions and guidance.

Improves relationships

Clarity in communication helps prevent confusion, frustration, and defensiveness. When everyone knows exactly what is expected, working relationships become smoother and more collaborative. It also fosters a positive environment where issues can be addressed openly and constructively.

Next-Level Skills

Enhances decision-making

When information is communicated clearly, it becomes easier for everyone to understand the situation and evaluate options. This leads to more effective problem-solving and better decisions, as people are able to think through issues with all the necessary facts at hand.

Drives accountability

Clear expectations and instructions make it much easier for people to take ownership of their responsibilities. When everyone understands what's required, individuals feel empowered and performance naturally improves because there is no ambiguity about what success looks like.

As Brené Brown puts it, very eloquently:

"Clear is kind. Unclear is unkind."

Practical Ways to Build Clear Communication

Clarity is a discipline.

It requires simplicity, structure, and empathy.

Simplicity means stripping away everything that doesn't serve your core message – every redundant word, every tangential thought, every impressive but unnecessary detail.

Structure provides the scaffolding that guides your audience from point A to point B without confusion, using logical flow and clear transitions.

Empathy is perhaps the most overlooked element: it requires stepping into your audience's shoes and asking what they need to know, what they already understand, and what might trip them up.

Let's look at practical ways to combine these three elements to bring in clarity.

Next-Level Skills

Step 1: Know Your Message

Before you speak or write, ask:

"What exactly do I want to say – and why?"

If you can't summarise your point in one sentence, you're not ready to share it yet.

Step 2: Simplify Your Language

Great communicators don't use big words – they use the *right* ones.

Replace jargon with meaning.

Shorten long sentences.

Clarity beats complexity, every time.

Next-Level Skills

Step 3: Structure Before You Speak

Order creates understanding.

Use this simple framework for verbal communication:

Context → Key Message → Call to Action.

For example:

"Here's what's happening, here's what it means, and here's what we'll do next."

Framing thoughts before speaking, gives your message the needed flow.

Step 4: Check for Understanding

Don't assume clarity – confirm it. Ask:

"Does that make sense?"

or

"What are your takeaways from this?"

Clarity isn't what you say – it's what they understand.

Next-Level Skills

Step 5: Match Words with Tone and Body Language

Nonverbal cues often speak louder than words.

Maintain open posture, consistent tone, and eye contact.

People don't just hear your message — they *feel* it.

Chapter 6: Clear Communication

Step 6: Communicate with Empathy

True clarity considers emotion as much as content.

Ask yourself:

"How might this message land for them?"

When you speak with empathy, you're not just transmitting information – you're building connection.

"Wise men speak because they have something to say. Fools because they have to say something."
– Plato

Next-Level Skills

Skill in Action: Real-World Examples

Barack Obama's Power of Precision and Pause

Barack Obama's public speaking style redefined modern political communication. In an age of noise and overstatement, his calm, measured delivery cut through with clarity. He often paused – letting ideas breathe before continuing. His speeches balanced intellect with accessibility, making complex issues relatable without oversimplifying them.

But behind the eloquence was discipline. Obama spent hours refining tone, rhythm, and word choice to ensure authenticity never got lost in polish. His clarity was born from empathy – the ability to meet people where they are. By saying less, he made every word count, proving that communication isn't about volume – it's about intention.

Clarity begins with the courage to slow down.

Brené Brown and the Language of Vulnerability

When researcher Brené Brown first spoke publicly about vulnerability, she expected discomfort, not virality. Yet her TED Talk on "The Power of Vulnerability" became one of the most viewed of all time. Her secret was simple: she didn't lecture – she conversed. She used plain language, self-deprecating humour, and storytelling to make emotional honesty accessible.

Her clarity came from speaking as a human, not an expert. By naming emotions that people often hide, she built bridges between psychology and everyday life. Brown's work reminds us that clear communication is not about polished delivery, but about the courage to speak truths simply and kindly.

Honesty is the most powerful form of clarity.

Simon Sinek's "Start With Why" Framework

Simon Sinek's now-famous TED Talk introduced a deceptively simple idea: people don't buy what you do, they buy *why* you do it. His clarity in expressing this concept turned it into a universal language for leadership. By drawing three circles on a whiteboard — Why, How, What — he reframed communication from the inside out.

The magic wasn't just the idea, but the way he communicated it: visual, structured, and emotionally anchored. He transformed abstract principles into memorable language, giving leaders everywhere a tool to articulate purpose. His example shows that clarity in communication often begins with clarity in thinking.

Simple words create lasting movements.

Chapter 6: Clear Communication

Gladys Berejiklian's Steady COVID-19 Communications

As Premier of New South Wales during the COVID-19 crisis, Gladys Berejiklian fronted daily press conferences, at exactly 11am Sydney time, every single day, weekday or weekend, where she addressed the public with measured composure and direct language.

Often flanked by health officials, Berejiklian provided regular updates, clarifying case numbers, restrictions, and health advice with a sense of urgency and straightforwardness. She balanced transparency about risks and setbacks with practical, actionable guidance for residents.

Her leadership style relied on *'without fail'* routine, reliability, consistency and clear articulation of evolving policies. By answering tough questions and acknowledging challenges, Berejiklian fostered a sense of shared responsibility, in difficult times.

Transparency transforms information into trust.

Next-Level Skills

Martin Luther King Jr.'s Dream with Direction

Martin Luther King Jr.'s "I Have a Dream" speech remains one of the clearest calls to human conscience in history. His choice of words was deliberate – simple enough for children to understand, powerful enough to move nations. He painted vivid pictures of justice and unity, turning ideals into imagery that everyone could feel.

Dr. King's clarity came from conviction. He didn't just communicate – he *channelled* purpose through poetry. His mastery of repetition, rhythm, and pause made his message unforgettable. True clarity, he showed, is when language lifts from the page and enters the heart.

Clarity is when words and purpose speak the same language.

Chapter 6: Clear Communication

Weekly Reflection Exercise

Take 10 quiet minutes to reflect on these:

How often do I assume I've communicated clearly without checking?

What's one situation recently where miscommunication caused friction?

How do I tend to communicate under stress – clearly or reactively?

Who around me models clarity well, and what can I learn from them?

Next-Level Skills

One Key Action Step This Week

Before your next important meeting or email, pause and ask:

"What's my core message — and what outcome do I want?"

Then say only what serves that goal.

Brevity is the secret to clarity.

Final Reflection

Clarity is not about saying more – it's about saying *what matters most*.

It's the foundation of trust, influence, and collaboration.

It makes ideas actionable, feedback digestible, and leadership relatable.

As Leonardo da Vinci observed:

"Simplicity is the ultimate sophistication."

Clear communication doesn't just express – it *connects*.

And that's how ideas move from mind to momentum.

Next-Level Skills

Chapter Immediately

Clear Communication

WHY IT MATTERS!

- ⭐ Saves time and reduces rework
- ⭐ Strengthens credibility
- ⭐ Improves relationships
- ⭐ Enhances decision-making
- ⭐ Drives accountability

PRACTICAL WAYS TO BUILD THE SKILL

1. Know Your Message

2. Simplify Your Language

3. Structure Before You Speak

4. Check for Understanding

5. Match Words with Tone and Body Language

6. Communicate with Empathy

Chapter 6: Clear Communication

Take It Further ...

- *How can simplifying your language improve your influence?*

- *What habits make your communication less clear, and how can you change them?*

- *How does empathy shape the way you communicate under pressure?*

- *In what ways can structure and brevity elevate your leadership presence?*

- *What's one conversation this week that deserves more clarity from you?*

- *How can visual or written summaries support clearer communication in your team?*

- *How do you balance honesty with kindness when communicating difficult messages?*

Next-Level Skills

Part III – The Human Connection: Building Trust and Collaboration

Adaptability sharpens your mind.
Strategic thinking broadens your vision.
Clear communication strengthens your voice.

By now, you've built the agility to navigate change with confidence – but leadership isn't a solo pursuit.

No matter how skilled or strategic we are, our impact depends on how well we connect with others.

Because success, at every level, is a *shared* space.

Next-Level Skills

The next stage of growth is about translating your personal mastery into *relational mastery*.

It's about trust — the quiet force that holds teams together through uncertainty.

Part III – *The Human Connection: Building Trust and Collaboration* – explores how to lead, influence, and resolve tension in ways that strengthen rather than strain relationships.

Here, you'll learn how to manage conflict with empathy, take accountability with integrity, and lead without needing authority.

Because leadership isn't about power — it's about partnership.

And when people feel seen, valued, and trusted, collaboration becomes unstoppable.

PART III
The Human Connection: Building Trust and Collaboration

07 — **Conflict Resolution**
Turning Friction into Forward Motion

08 — **Accountability**
Owning the Outcome – Not Just the Effort

09 — **Leadership Without Authority**
Influence Without a Title

"Relationships are the real currency of leadership"

Next-Level Skills

Chapter 7: Conflict Resolution

"Turning Friction into Forward Motion"

Next-Level Skills

Building on *Clear Communication*, conflict resolution is where understanding meets courage.

It's the skill that transforms disagreement into dialogue – and tension into trust.

Conflict isn't the enemy of progress – silence is!

When managed with awareness and empathy, conflict becomes one of the most powerful tools for growth, innovation, and stronger relationships.

Chapter 7: Conflict Resolution

"The Meeting That Changed Everything"

A senior product team in Atlanta was stuck.

Two department heads had been in quiet disagreement for months – one wanted to prioritise speed, the other insisted on quality.

Meetings became battles of tone and timing.

Deadlines slipped. Morale sank.

Finally, the CEO called a joint session and said one thing:

"We're not here to prove who's right. We're here to understand why we both care."

That sentence shifted the energy instantly.

By the end of the meeting, both leaders realised their goals weren't opposites – they were complementary.

Next-Level Skills

Speed mattered to get feedback early. Quality mattered to deliver excellence.

The result?

A new, shared process that improved both metrics.

Conflict didn't destroy alignment – it *created* it.

"Peace is not the absence of conflict, but the ability to cope with it."
– Mahatma Gandhi

Chapter 7: Conflict Resolution

Why Conflict Resolution Matters

Every strong relationship – personal or professional – faces friction.

The difference between dysfunction and growth lies in *how* you manage it.

Conflict is not the problem. Avoidance and poor handling are. When tensions arise and people pretend everything is fine, resentment accumulates like compound interest, quietly eroding trust until relationships collapse under the weight of unspoken grievances.

Conversely, when conflict is addressed with skill and courage, it becomes a clarifying force – exposing misalignments, surfacing hidden needs, and creating opportunities for deeper understanding.

The most resilient teams and partnerships aren't those that never disagree. They're the ones that have learned to navigate disagreement productively and working through friction together.

Next-Level Skills

Here's why resolving conflicts matters:

Conflict Resolution
Why It Matters!

1	Builds trust through transparency
2	Encourages innovation
3	Reduces workplace stress
4	Improves decision quality
5	Strengthens leadership credibility

Builds trust through transparency

Open, honest discussion lays the foundation for strong relationships within teams. When people feel safe to express their thoughts and concerns, it creates an environment of mutual respect and reliability. Transparency ensures that misunderstandings are addressed before they can fester, deepening trust among colleagues.

Encourages innovation

Welcoming a range of diverse perspectives often sparks creative tension, which is a catalyst for new ideas and breakthroughs. When team members feel empowered to challenge assumptions and propose alternative solutions, it leads to more robust problem-solving and drives innovation across projects and processes.

Reduces workplace stress

Proactively addressing issues as they arise prevents resentment from building up over time. By resolving small disagreements early, teams avoid escalation into bigger problems, which contributes to a more harmonious and supportive workplace in the long run. This reduction in stress helps individuals remain focused and productive.

Improves decision quality

Healthy debate encourages team members to consider different viewpoints, leading to a deeper and more thorough understanding of the issues at hand. As a result, decisions are made with greater insight and are more likely to stand up to scrutiny, benefitting the organisation, as a whole.

Strengthens leadership credibility

Great leaders demonstrate their ability to manage differences without damaging respect among their team members. By addressing conflict constructively and fairly, leaders earn the trust and confidence of others, reinforcing their reputation for integrity and professionalism.

Chapter 7: Conflict Resolution

As Patrick Lencioni, author of *The Five Dysfunctions of a Team*, noted:

"Teams that fear conflict have meetings that are boring and ineffective."

Healthy conflict is a sign of engagement – not dysfunction.

Next-Level Skills

Practical Ways to Build Conflict Resolution Skills

Conflict resolution blends emotional intelligence, active listening, and clear communication.

Emotional intelligence helps you recognize when your own triggers are clouding judgment and enables you to read the emotional undercurrents in others, so you're always responding to the real issue at hand.

Active listening transforms adversaries into collaborators by creating space where all parties feel genuinely heard, which often dissolves defensiveness before solutions are even discussed.

Clear communication ensures that what you mean is what they understand, preventing the secondary conflicts that arise from misinterpretation.

Mastering conflict requires more than good intentions – it demands a toolkit of specific skills working in harmony. Let's look at steps to make it happen.

Step 1: Redefine Conflict

Start by reframing it.

Conflict isn't a fight – it's feedback.

Ask yourself:

"What is this disagreement trying to teach us?"

Seeing conflict as data lowers defensiveness.

Next-Level Skills

Step 2: Separate People from Problems

Attack the issue, not the individual.

Use phrases like

"The challenge we're facing is..." instead of *"You always..."*

This small shift keeps conversations constructive, not personal.

Step 3: Listen to Understand Before Responding

Before defending your position, summarise the other person's. Say,

"It sounds like your main concern is..."

Feeling heard defuses emotion faster than logic ever can.

Next-Level Skills

Step 4: Identify Shared Goals

Conflict resolution isn't about compromise – it's about alignment. Ask:

"What outcome do we both want?"

Most disagreements shrink when viewed through a shared purpose.

Step 5: Manage Emotions, Not Just Arguments

Pause when tension rises.

Take a breath.

Slow your tone.

Model calm – it's contagious.

Emotional composure is the foundation of resolution.

Next-Level Skills

Step 6: Follow Up After Resolution

The conversation isn't over when the meeting ends.

Revisit agreements, check progress, and reinforce trust.

Follow-up turns temporary peace into lasting collaboration.

"In any moment of conflict, the first to listen wins."
– *Unknown*

Chapter 7: Conflict Resolution

Skill in Action: Real-World Examples

Nelson Mandela and the Art of Reconciliation

When Nelson Mandela became South Africa's president in 1994, he faced a nation fractured by decades of apartheid. Many expected retributions. Instead, Mandela chose reconciliation. He invited his former jailers to his inauguration and supported the Truth and Reconciliation Commission – a forum where victims and perpetrators could share stories publicly. His 'shocking' decision healed a nation.

Mandela understood that peace required more than forgiveness - it required truth. By facing pain directly and turning vengeance into understanding, he modelled a rare kind of strength: the courage to prioritise healing over victory. His leadership transformed conflict resolution into nation's empathy.

Resolution begins where revenge ends.

Next-Level Skills

Abraham Lincoln's "Team of Rivals" Leadership

When Abraham Lincoln became U.S. president, he filled his cabinet with political opponents – people who had criticised, doubted, and even opposed him. Instead of surrounding himself with loyalists, Lincoln valued dissent. He believed that constructive conflict, managed with humility, produced stronger decisions.

He often mediated intense disagreements by listening patiently, seeking middle ground without abandoning principle. This approach turned rivalry into respect and unity into strength. Lincoln's leadership shows that the best way to resolve conflict is to invite it – not to avoid it – and to use it as a forge for better thinking.

Great leaders don't silence conflict. They channel it.

Chapter 7: Conflict Resolution

Mahatma Gandhi's Nonviolent Resistance

Gandhi's philosophy of *Ahimsa* – nonviolence – was not passive tolerance but active resistance through peace. He believed that truth and compassion could dismantle oppression more powerfully than force. In leading India's independence movement, Gandhi transformed confrontation into dialogue, and hostility into awakening.

His marches, hunger strikes, and peaceful protests demonstrated moral courage rooted in empathy. Gandhi's genius lay in separating the person from the problem – opposing injustice without dehumanising the unjust. His life proved that resolving conflict sometimes requires endurance, not aggression.

Peaceful strength is the highest form of power.

Next-Level Skills

Satya Nadella's Empathy in Organisational Conflict

When Satya Nadella took over as Microsoft CEO, he inherited a culture marked by internal competition and silos. We had investigated this example for exploring skills like Self-awareness and Emotional Intelligence as well, in previous chapters.

Rather than enforcing compliance, he created safe spaces for disagreement. Nadella encouraged teams to challenge ideas, not individuals, shifting focus from blame to learning. By listening deeply and validating different perspectives, he transformed conflict into innovation.

Under his leadership, debates became constructive dialogues. Microsoft's shift from a "know-it-all" to a "learn-it-all" culture proved that empathy and curiosity resolve more conflicts than authority ever could.

Empathy turns conflict into collaboration.

Ruth Bader Ginsburg's Respectful Dissent

Justice Ruth Bader Ginsburg spent decades on the U.S. Supreme Court, often dissenting passionately from the majority. Yet, even when her opinions opposed her colleagues, she maintained deep personal friendships – including with Justice Antonin Scalia, her ideological opposite. Their mutual respect became legendary, showing that fierce disagreement need not destroy connection.

Ginsburg approached conflict with grace and reason. She saw dissent as dialogue – a way to sharpen democracy, not fracture it. Her legacy reminds us that the goal of resolution isn't uniformity, but understanding rooted in respect.

Respect sustains dialogue long after agreement fades.

Next-Level Skills

Weekly Reflection Exercise

Take 10 quiet minutes to reflect on these:

How do I typically respond to conflict – fight, flight, or freeze?

When was the last time I avoided a necessary difficult conversation?

What does a "healthy disagreement" look like to me?

How can I bring curiosity instead of defensiveness into my next tense discussion?

Chapter 7: Conflict Resolution

One Key Action Step This Week

Have one *small but honest* conversation you've been avoiding.

Start with empathy, not accusation:

"I'd like to understand your perspective better – can we talk about it?"

Courage doesn't eliminate conflict.

It transforms it.

Final Reflection

Conflict isn't a threat to unity – it's a test of maturity.

When managed well, it builds stronger teams, deeper trust, and better decisions.

It's the friction that sharpens ideas and the dialogue that deepens respect.

As Martin Luther King Jr. said:

"We must learn to live together as brothers or perish together as fools."

The goal isn't to avoid conflict – it's to master it.

Because on the other side of every honest conversation lies progress.

Chapter 7: Conflict Resolution

Chapter Immediately

Conflict Resolution

WHY IT MATTERS!

- Builds trust through transparency
- Encourages innovation
- Reduces workplace stress
- Improves decision quality
- Strengthens leadership credibility

PRACTICAL WAYS TO BUILD THE SKILL

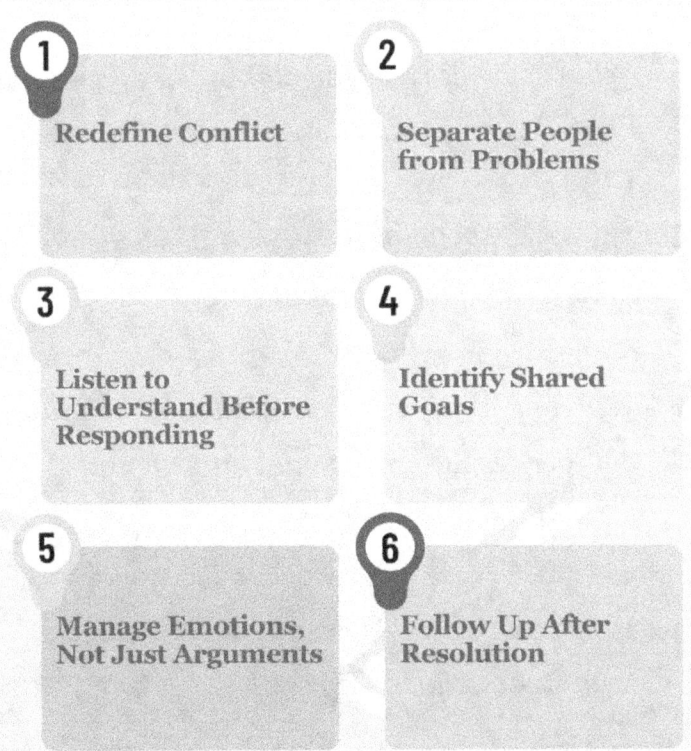

1. Redefine Conflict
2. Separate People from Problems
3. Listen to Understand Before Responding
4. Identify Shared Goals
5. Manage Emotions, Not Just Arguments
6. Follow Up After Resolution

Next-Level Skills

Take It Further ...

- *What patterns do you notice in how you typically manage conflict?*

- *Which relationships in your life could benefit from more open dialogue?*

- *How can you ensure emotions don't override your message during tension?*

- *What's one phrase you can use to de-escalate heated discussions?*

- *How can feedback conversations become more about learning than blame?*

- *Who in your team or circle models healthy conflict resolution – and what can you emulate?*

- *How can you foster a culture that values honesty and harmony?*

Chapter 8: Accountability

"Owning the Outcome – Not Just the Effort"

Next-Level Skills

Building on *Conflict Resolution*, accountability is what transforms conversations into commitments.

It's the difference between *saying* and *doing*, between intention and integrity.

When conflict is resolved and expectations are clear, accountability ensures follow-through – it's what keeps promises from fading into good intentions.

Accountability isn't about blame. It's about *ownership*.

It's not about perfection.

It's about responsibility.

In high-performing teams – and fulfilling lives – accountability is the glue that holds trust together.

Chapter 8: Accountability

"The Power of One Honest Question"

A senior operations manager once shared a story about a project that went off track.

Timelines slipped.

Costs crept up.

Deadlines were missed.

When the dust settled, she gathered her team and asked just one question:

"What part of this outcome do I own?"

That question changed the conversation from *finger-pointing* to *problem-solving*.

Each person identified one thing they could have done differently – from clearer handovers to better follow-ups.

Next-Level Skills

Within weeks, the same team was performing stronger than ever.

Accountability didn't come from punishment – it came from reflection.

"Accountability breeds response-ability."
– Stephen R. Covey

Chapter 8: Accountability

Why Accountability Matters

Accountability is the cornerstone of trust. Without it, even the best strategies collapse under inconsistency.

When people do what they say they'll do, relationships strengthen and momentum builds. When they don't, credibility erodes faster than it can be rebuilt.

Accountability isn't about blame or punishment – it's about ownership and follow-through. It means being answerable for your commitments, transparent about your progress, and honest when you fall short.

In organizations, lack of accountability creates a culture where deadlines are suggestions, standards are negotiable, and responsibility diffuses into the ether with everyone pointing fingers and no one stepping up.

The leaders and colleagues who inspire the most loyalty aren't necessarily the most talented – they're the ones who consistently show up and deliver, modelling the reliability they expect from others.

Next-Level Skills

Here's why being accountable matters:

Accountability
Why It Matters!

1	**Builds reliability and credibility**
2	**Creates clarity**
3	**Drives performance**
4	**Encourages learning**
5	**Strengthens culture**

Builds reliability and credibility

When people consistently follow through on their commitments, others know they can be counted on. Over time, this reliability fosters trust and a strong reputation for credibility within the team and organisation.

Creates clarity

Taking ownership eliminates confusion about roles and responsibilities. When everyone knows exactly who is responsible for what, tasks don't fall through the cracks and teams can operate more efficiently.

Drives performance

Accountability doesn't just keep people on track, it turns goals into clear, measurable outcomes. By making expectations explicit and holding each other to them, teams are more likely to achieve – and even exceed – their targets.

Next-Level Skills

Encourages learning

When mistakes happen, accountability shifts the focus from blame to improvement. Individuals and teams can reflect on what went wrong, extract valuable lessons, and apply those insights to do better next time.

Strengthens culture

A culture of accountability ensures everyone is committed to contributing their fair share. When all team members pull their own weight, it fosters mutual respect, boosts morale, and helps the team achieve shared success.

Chapter 8: Accountability

As Brené Brown reminds us:

"*Daring leaders must care for people and hold them accountable for their behaviours.*"

Accountability isn't harsh – it's healthy.

It's how individuals grow and teams stay aligned.

Next-Level Skills

Practical Ways to Build Accountability

Accountability is built through consistency, transparency, and follow-through.

Consistency means your actions align with your words not just once, but repeatedly over time – it's the pattern that proves reliability.

Transparency involves being open about your progress, your setbacks, and your decision-making process, so others aren't left guessing or filling gaps with doubt.

Follow-through is the non-negotiable finish line: completing what you started, closing the loop, and honouring commitments even when enthusiasm fades or obstacles emerge.

These three elements form an unbreakable chain to transform accountability into a visible behaviour. Let's learn practical ways to practice these elements.

Step 1: Define Clear Expectations

You can't hold people accountable for what they don't understand.

Agree on *who does what by when.*

Ambiguity is the enemy of accountability.

Next-Level Skills

Step 2: Set Measurable Outcomes

Replace vague goals with concrete results.

Not *"Do your best,"*

but *"Deliver X by Friday."*

Clarity makes accountability measurable – and fair.

Step 3: Model It Yourself

Leaders can't demand what they don't demonstrate.

Own your mistakes publicly.

Follow through visibly.

Accountability cascades from example, not enforcement.

Next-Level Skills

Step 4: Create Check-Ins, Not Check-Ups

Regular reviews aren't about policing – they're about progress. Ask:

"What's working?

What's stuck?

What support do you need?"

Frequent dialogue keeps accountability alive without fear.

Step 5: Address Gaps Early

When commitments slip, act fast and fairly. Ask:

"Help me understand what happened and how we can fix it?"

Ignoring small lapses sends a loud message – that standards don't matter.

Next-Level Skills

Step 6: Celebrate Ownership

Acknowledge those who take responsibility — even for mistakes.

Recognition turns accountability into pride, not punishment.

"Leaders inspire accountability through their ability to accept responsibility before they place blame."

— *Courtney Lynch*

Chapter 8: Accountability

Skill in Action: Real-World Examples

J&J and the Tylenol Crisis Response

In 1982, seven people in Chicago died after taking cyanide-laced Tylenol capsules. It was a nightmare scenario for Johnson & Johnson – a trusted household brand suddenly associated with tragedy. The company could have deflected blame, but instead, CEO James Burke acted decisively. He recalled 31 million bottles nationwide, halted production, and prioritised public safety over profit.

This transparent and costly move, guided by the company's credo – "the needs of the people we serve come first" – restored public confidence and reshaped industry standards for safety. By taking responsibility instead of hiding behind uncertainty, Johnson & Johnson turned crisis into credibility.

Accountability builds trust faster than perfection ever could.

Next-Level Skills

General Dwight D. Eisenhower and the D-Day Letter

On the eve of the D-Day invasion in 1944, General Eisenhower wrote two letters: one announcing victory and another accepting full responsibility in case of failure. "If any blame or fault attaches to the attempt," he wrote, "it is mine alone." That letter, never sent, captured the spirit of accountability in leadership – ownership without excuses.

Eisenhower's mindset set the tone for his troops: that true command means bearing the weight of outcomes, not sharing it selectively. His integrity became a moral compass, showing that accountability isn't declared after results – it's embraced before them.

Accountability means owning the risk, not just the reward.

Chapter 8: Accountability

Serena Williams and Taking Ownership of Emotion

In a 2018 U.S. Open final marked by controversy, Serena Williams' confrontation with an umpire drew global attention. Later, she publicly reflected on her reaction – acknowledging her intensity while reaffirming her values. Her openness to examine her emotions and behaviour in the global spotlight turned criticism into conversation about fairness, gender, and respect.

By not dismissing the moment but owning her part in it, she modelled maturity and leadership. Serena's accountability extended beyond performance – it was personal, showing that integrity isn't the absence of emotion but the courage to learn from it.

Accountability begins where defensiveness ends.

Next-Level Skills

Patagonia's Environmental Accountability

Outdoor brand Patagonia has long tied its mission to environmental responsibility. When founder Yvon Chouinard announced in 2022 that he was giving away the company to fight climate change, he said, "Earth is now our only shareholder." This wasn't a marketing move – it was a radical act of accountability to the planet that sustained their success.

Patagonia's consistency – from transparent supply chains to repair programs – shows that accountability can be expansive, extending beyond profit to purpose. It's a reminder that responsibility doesn't limit ambition – it defines legacy.

Accountability to purpose outlasts accountability to profit.

Chapter 8: Accountability

NASA's Challenger Disaster and the Power of Admitting Failure

When the Space Shuttle Challenger exploded in 1986, killing seven astronauts, the tragedy exposed communication failures and systemic pressure within NASA. Instead of concealment, the Rogers Commission publicly investigated the causes. Engineers and leaders testified about ignored warnings, creating a culture of transparency that reshaped NASA's safety practices.

The organisation's willingness to face hard truths – at the cost of reputation – laid the foundation for reform and renewed trust. NASA's evolution from denial to disclosure became one of the most powerful lessons in collective accountability in history.

Owning mistakes is the first step towards restoring integrity.

Next-Level Skills

Weekly Reflection Exercise

Take 10 quiet minutes to reflect on these:

When things go wrong, do I look outward or inward first?

How clear are my own commitments — to others and to myself?

What habits help me stay consistent with what I say I'll do?

How can I model accountability in small, everyday ways?

Chapter 8: Accountability

One Key Action Step This Week

Identify one recurring responsibility you've been postponing.

Take one visible step towards completing it – and tell someone you trust about it.

Accountability grows strongest in the light of visibility.

Next-Level Skills

Final Reflection

Accountability isn't about control – it's about commitment.

It's what transforms teams from compliant to committed, and individuals from reactive to dependable.

When people consistently own their outcomes, trust compounds – and performance follows.

As John G. Miller wrote:

"The question is not 'Who is accountable?' The question is 'Am I?'"

Accountability doesn't limit freedom – it *amplifies* it, because it gives everyone the confidence to depend on each other.

That's the essence of integrity in action.

Chapter 8: Accountability

Chapter Immediately

Accountability

WHY IT MATTERS!

- Builds reliability and credibility
- Creates clarity
- Drives performance
- Encourages learning
- Strengthens culture

PRACTICAL WAYS TO BUILD THE SKILL

1. Define Clear Expectations

2. Set Measurable Outcomes

3. Model It Yourself

4. Create Check-Ins, Not Check-Ups

5. Address Gaps Early

6. Celebrate Ownership

Next-Level Skills

Take It Further ...

- How do you currently define accountability – and how might you redefine it?

- Where in your work or life do you need to be more transparent about ownership?

- How can you encourage accountability without creating fear?

- What's one system or ritual that would help your team follow through better?

- How do you personally recover when you drop the ball?

- Who do you admire for their sense of ownership and what can you learn from them?

- How does accountability connect with trust and performance in your team culture?

Chapter 8: Accountability

- *What are some barriers – internal or external – that make it challenging to practise accountability, and how can you address them?*

- *How do you communicate expectations around accountability in your team or organisation?*

- *What role does feedback play in fostering a culture of accountability, and how can you ensure it's constructive?*

Next-Level Skills

Chapter 9: Leadership Without Authority

"Influence Without a Title"

Next-Level Skills

Building on *Accountability*, leadership without authority is about stepping up before you're asked to.

It's leading through *credibility, character,* and *connection* – not position or power.

In modern workplaces, leadership isn't confined to corner offices. It happens in conversations, in collaboration, and in the quiet choices people make to take responsibility when they don't have to.

Because real leaders don't wait for permission to make a difference.

They lead from where they are.

Chapter 9: Leadership Without Authority

"The Analyst Who Changed the Culture"

At a large financial services firm, a mid-level analyst noticed a recurring issue: teams weren't sharing information across departments.

Projects overlapped, deadlines clashed, and opportunities were missed.

Instead of complaining, he started small.

He organised a weekly "Cross-Team Coffee Chat" – a casual 15-minute sync where anyone could share updates.

Within months, silos started to break down.

Collaboration improved.

Senior managers took notice and expanded his idea company-wide.

Next-Level Skills

He didn't have a leadership title – but he had *leadership impact*.

His influence didn't come from authority.

It came from initiative.

"You don't need a title to be a leader."
– Robin Sharma

Chapter 9: Leadership Without Authority

Why Leadership Without Authority Matters

The future belongs to those who can influence without control.

In matrix organisations, project-based work, and hybrid teams, authority is often distributed – but leadership must be multiplied.

Gone are the days when leadership meant commanding from the top of a clear hierarchy. Today's most effective leaders operate in ambiguous spaces where they must inspire action without formal power, align diverse stakeholders without direct authority, and drive results through people who don't report to them.

This requires a fundamentally different skill set: the ability to build coalitions rather than issue orders, to persuade through vision rather than mandate through position, and to earn followership through credibility rather than demand it through title.

Next-Level Skills

Here's why leading without authority matters:

Leadership Without Authority
Why It Matters!

1	**Empowers everyone**
2	**Builds trust and collaboration**
3	**Encourages innovation**
4	**Develops future leaders**
5	**Creates resilience**

Empowers everyone

When individuals are encouraged to lead from their current roles, regardless of their position or title, the whole team becomes more agile and responsive. This sense of empowerment allows people to speak up, contribute ideas, and take initiative, which helps teams adapt quickly to new challenges and opportunities.

Builds trust and collaboration

True influence is earned through credibility, reliability, and authentic relationships, not simply from holding a particular spot in the organisational hierarchy. When team members see each other consistently delivering on commitments and listening to one another, trust deepens and collaboration flourishes, creating a supportive environment where everyone feels valued.

Encourages innovation

By giving people, the freedom to act on their ideas, you foster a culture where creativity and experimentation thrive. Instead of waiting for approval from above, team members are motivated to propose solutions, assess new approaches, and take calculated risks, which leads to fresh thinking and continuous improvement.

Develops future leaders

When initiative is recognised and encouraged, it becomes the natural starting point for developing future leaders within the organisation. Those who step up and demonstrate leadership qualities, regardless of their official role, gain valuable experience and confidence that prepares them for more formal leadership positions down the track.

Creates resilience

Sharing leadership across a team spreads responsibility and reduces the burden that might otherwise fall on a single person. This collective approach ensures that when unexpected challenges arise, the team can draw upon a wider pool of perspectives, skills, and strengths, helping everyone to

Chapter 9: Leadership Without Authority

navigate uncertainty and bounce back more effectively.

As leadership expert, John Maxwell says:

"Leadership is influence – nothing more, nothing less."

Next-Level Skills

Practical Ways to Lead Without Authority

Leading without authority is about presence, not position.

It's about showing up with such clarity, competence, and conviction that people choose to follow you regardless of what your business card says.

Presence means being fully engaged, radiating confidence without arrogance, and demonstrating through your actions that you're worth listening to. It's the quiet authority that comes from knowing your craft, honouring your commitments, and treating others with respect.

When you lead through presence, you don't need a title to command attention or permission to make an impact – your contribution speaks for itself, and people naturally gravitate toward the value you bring.

Here are six powerful ways to do it.

Chapter 9: Leadership Without Authority

Step 1: Build Trust Through Reliability

People follow consistency more than charisma.

Do what you say, deliver on time, and be dependable.

Trust is your first and strongest form of authority.

Next-Level Skills

Step 2: Master the Art of Listening

When you listen deeply, people feel valued and they'll follow your lead willingly.

Asking good questions and reflecting understanding earns you influence faster than giving orders.

Step 3: Influence Through Expertise

Become known for something.

Whether it's technical depth, communication, or problem-solving – be the person others come to for insight.

Expertise gives you a voice even without a title.

Next-Level Skills

Step 4: Elevate Others

Great informal leaders lift others up.

Share credit.

Celebrate contributions.

When you make others look good, your influence multiplies naturally.

Step 5: Communicate with Confidence and Respect

You don't need authority to speak up, but you do need tact.

Use assertive, not aggressive, communication.

Say what needs to be said – clearly, calmly, and constructively.

Step 6: Model the Behaviours You Want to See

Culture changes one action at a time.

Be the example.

Show integrity, curiosity, and accountability.

Influence begins when people watch what you do, not what you say.

"Example is leadership."
– Albert Schweitzer

Chapter 9: Leadership Without Authority

Skill in Action: Real-World Examples

Malala Yousafzai's Global Advocacy for Education

At just 15, Malala Yousafzai was not a politician, a CEO, or an official leader. Yet her courage to speak publicly for girls' education in Pakistan made her a global symbol of change. Even after surviving an assassination attempt, she chose dialogue over vengeance. Without holding any formal power, she influenced world leaders, shaped policies, and inspired a generation to view education as a right.

Malala's story illustrates that true leadership doesn't require permission – it requires conviction. Her strength lies in her moral authority, not positional authority. Through grace and determination, she showed that voice can be more powerful than title.

Influence grows strongest when it serves a purpose greater than self.

Next-Level Skills

Rosa Parks and the Quiet Act that Moved a Nation

On December 1, 1955, Rosa Parks refused to give up her seat on a Montgomery bus. It was a small act of defiance that sparked a movement. Parks wasn't a public figure. She was a seamstress with quiet resolve. Yet that simple, courageous decision triggered the Montgomery Bus Boycott – one of the pivotal moments of the American civil rights movement.

Her leadership came not from authority, but from authenticity. Parks' moral clarity mobilised thousands, including Dr. Martin Luther King Jr., proving that sometimes leadership begins in stillness – a single act of conscience that ripples across history.

Leadership begins the moment you decide not to wait for permission.

Chapter 9: Leadership Without Authority

Greta Thunberg and Youth-Led Climate Action

In 2018, a 15-year-old student from Sweden began skipping school on Fridays to protest climate inaction outside her parliament. Within months, Greta Thunberg's solitary act became a global youth movement. Without formal backing or institutional authority, she addressed the United Nations, challenging world leaders with unflinching honesty.

Her leadership style – blunt, uncompromising, and grounded in truth – disrupted global complacency. Greta proved that influence today is no longer confined to hierarchy. It belongs to those with clarity, conviction, and courage to speak when others stay silent.

Leadership without authority is the art of leading through truth.

Next-Level Skills

Edward Snowden and the Ethics of Speaking Up

In 2013, Edward Snowden, a contractor for the U.S. National Security Agency, made one of the most controversial decisions in modern history – leaking classified documents to expose mass surveillance programs. Regardless of opinion about his methods, Snowden's choice was an act of individual conscience that reshaped the global conversation on privacy and ethics.

Without institutional backing, he risked his freedom to hold power accountable. His story embodies the uncomfortable truth of leadership without authority: that sometimes, responsibility demands action even when protection is absent.

Leadership without title is often leadership with risk.

Chapter 9: Leadership Without Authority

Desmond Tutu's Moral Leadership in Post-Apartheid South Africa

As chair of South Africa's Truth and Reconciliation Commission, Archbishop Desmond Tutu wielded moral, not political, authority. He created a sacred space where victims and perpetrators of apartheid could tell their stories. His laughter, tears, and faith turned the process from bureaucracy into healing.

Tutu's influence stemmed from integrity and humanity, not hierarchy. His compassion guided a divided nation towards forgiveness. His legacy proves that authority may grant control – but only character grants influence.

True authority is earned through integrity, not imposed through power.

Leadership isn't a position. It's a posture.

Next-Level Skills

Weekly Reflection Exercise

Take 10 quiet minutes to reflect on these:

Where am I waiting for permission to lead – and why?

What strengths can I use right now to positively influence my team?

Who in my workplace leads without a title – and what can I learn from them?

How can I make a difference this week without needing formal authority?

Chapter 9: Leadership Without Authority

One Key Action Step This Week

Identify one small initiative that would improve collaboration, morale, or workflow – and take action.

It could be a shared document, a check-in ritual, or a new idea forum.

Don't wait for a title – just start.

Leadership happens the moment you take responsibility beyond your role.

Next-Level Skills

Final Reflection

True leadership has nothing to do with rank and everything to do with impact.

It's not about control – it's about contribution.

Not about being in charge – but about caring enough to make things better.

As Simon Sinek said:

"Leadership is not about being in charge. It's about taking care of those in your charge."

When you lead without authority, you embody the highest form of influence – the kind that inspires others to do the same.

That's leadership that lasts.

Chapter 9: Leadership Without Authority

Chapter Immediately

Leadership Without Authority

WHY IT MATTERS!

- ⭐ Empowers everyone
- ⭐ Builds trust and collaboration
- ⭐ Encourages innovation
- ⭐ Develops future leaders
- ⭐ Creates resilience

PRACTICAL WAYS TO BUILD THE SKILL

1. Build Trust Through Reliability

2. Master the Art of Listening

3. Influence Through Expertise

4. Elevate Others

5. Communicate with Confidence and Respect

6. Model the Behaviours You Want to See

Next-Level Skills

Take It Further ...

- *What does "leading from where you are" mean to you personally?*

- *How can you grow credibility and trust in your current role?*

- *How does empathy strengthen your ability to influence others?*

- *What's one barrier stopping you from stepping up, and how can you remove it?*

- *How can you encourage others to lead, even without formal authority?*

- *What daily habits can you develop to reinforce your leadership mindset, regardless of your position?*

- *How can you create opportunities for others to contribute their strengths within your team or community?*

Chapter 9: Leadership Without Authority

- *In what ways can you seek feedback to continuously improve your influence and impact?*

- *How do you balance assertiveness with collaboration when leading without formal power?*

- *What small action can you take today to demonstrate leadership in a situation where you have no direct control?*

Next-Level Skills

Part IV – The Growth Continuum: Sustaining Purpose and Impact

By now, you've learned to lead with empathy, resolve conflict with courage, and take ownership without waiting for authority.

You've seen how trust transforms teams and how influence begins long before titles do.

But the true test of leadership isn't found in moments of success – it's found in moments of strain.

When the pace quickens, the pressure rises, and the path ahead feels uncertain, what keeps you steady?

That's where the final stage of growth begins.

Next-Level Skills

Part IV – *The Growth Continuum: Sustaining Purpose and Impact* – is about endurance, direction, and legacy.

It explores how to stay grounded when challenged (*Resilience*), how to channel strength into intention (*Personal Goal Setting*), and how to communicate meaning in ways that move others (*Storytelling for Influence*).

These final chapters are about building a leadership practice that lasts – one rooted not just in skill, but in purpose.

Because mastering yourself and leading others are only the beginning.

Sustaining both – with clarity, resilience, and meaning – is where true next-level leadership lives.

PART IV
The Growth Continuum: Sustaining Purpose and Impact

10   **Resilience**
Bending Without Breaking

11   **Personal Goal Setting**
Direction Over Distraction

12   **Storytelling for Influence**
Turning Insight into Impact

"True growth is built on resilience, clarity, and meaning"

Next-Level Skills

Chapter 10: Resilience

"Bending Without Breaking"

Next-Level Skills

Building on *Leadership Without Authority*, resilience is the quiet strength that keeps you standing when everything around you, shakes.

It's not about being tough all the time – it's about recovering quickly, learning deeply, and continuing bravely.

Resilience doesn't mean ignoring challenges. It means facing them with perspective and purpose.

Because growth doesn't happen in the calm – it happens in the comeback.

Chapter 10: Resilience

"The Day Everything Fell Apart"

A project manager at a construction firm in Dubai had been leading a major initiative for nearly a year.

Then, just two weeks before delivery, a critical subcontractor failed to meet their obligations.

The schedule collapsed.

The client was furious.

The stress was enormous.

In that moment, she had two choices: panic or pause.

She gathered her team, acknowledged the setback honestly, and said:

"We can't control what happened – but we can control how we respond."

They reorganised tasks, prioritised critical deliverables, and pulled together instead of falling

Next-Level Skills

apart.

The project still finished – two weeks late, but with a team that was stronger, prouder, and more unified than ever before.

That's resilience in motion – grace under pressure, and growth through challenge.

"It's your reaction to adversity, not adversity itself, that determines how your life's story will develop."
– Dieter F. Uchtdorf

Chapter 10: Resilience

Why Resilience Matters

In a world of constant change, resilience isn't optional – it's essential.

It's what allows you to adapt without losing focus, persist without burning out, and lead without fear.

Resilience is the shock absorber between disruption and breakdown. It's not about being invincible or never feeling the weight of pressure – it's about bouncing back stronger each time life knocks you down.

Resilient people don't avoid difficulty. They metabolize it, extracting lessons from failure and fuel from adversity. They maintain perspective when chaos swirls around them, recognizing that setbacks are temporary and challenges are surmountable.

This quality separates those who crumble under stress from those who rise through it, transforming obstacles into stepping stones.

Next-Level Skills

Here's why resilience matters:

Resilience
Why It Matters!

1	**Builds stability under stress**
2	**Enables faster recovery**
3	**Strengthens confidence**
4	**Inspires others**
5	**Supports sustained success**

Chapter 10: Resilience

Builds stability under stress

When the pressure rises and circumstances become uncertain, resilience helps you remain calm, composed, and resourceful while others may feel overwhelmed or panic. It allows you to think clearly, make sound decisions, and guide others through turbulent times.

Enables faster recovery

Resilience lets you not only bounce back from setbacks but also bounce forward. Instead of being held back by adversity, you use challenges as a springboard for learning, personal growth, and renewed motivation, returning stronger than before.

Strengthens confidence

Each time you overcome obstacles, your belief in your own abilities grows. You develop trust in yourself to manage hard things, which builds a deep-seated confidence that carries over into future challenges and opportunities.

Inspires others

Your steadiness and positive response to adversity serve as an example for those around you. When you show resilience, you give others the courage to persevere, strengthening the team's collective spirit and resolve.

Supports sustained success

Without resilience, even the most talented people can burn out or lose direction. Resilience underpins long-term achievement by helping you maintain your enthusiasm, energy, and wellbeing through both the highs and lows of any journey.

As Viktor Frankl wrote in *Man's Search for Meaning*:

"When we are no longer able to change a situation, we are challenged to change ourselves."

Chapter 10: Resilience

Practical Ways to Build Resilience

Resilience isn't an inherited trait – it's a skill you strengthen daily.

The myth that some people are simply "born resilient" while others aren't, does a profound disservice to human potential. Resilience emerges from specific behaviours, thought patterns, and practices that anyone can cultivate with intention.

It's built through small, repeated choices: how you interpret setbacks, where you direct your attention, how you care for your physical and mental well-being, and who you surround yourself with.

Like building muscle at the gym, developing resilience requires consistent effort over time – you don't become unshakeable overnight, but each challenge you navigate effectively compounds your capacity.

Let's look into practical ways to keep compounding resilience.

Next-Level Skills

Step 1: Reframe Setbacks as Setups

When things go wrong, resist the urge to label them as failure.

Ask instead:

"What is this teaching me?"

Every challenge carries a hidden gift of insight.

Chapter 10: Resilience

Step 2: Regulate Your Energy, Not Just Your Emotions

Rest, nutrition, and movement are not indulgences – they're foundations of resilience.

A depleted body can't sustain a strong mind.

Protect your energy like your most valuable resource – because it is!

Next-Level Skills

Step 3: Anchor to Purpose

When pressure mounts, clarity of purpose becomes your compass. Ask:

"Why does this matter?"

Purpose gives meaning to struggle and transforms obstacles into endurance.

Chapter 10: Resilience

Step 4: Build a Support Network

Resilience isn't a solo performance.

Lean on trusted mentors, colleagues, or friends.

Connection replenishes courage.

Step 5: Embrace Micro-Recovery

Take small moments to reset – a walk, a breath, a pause between meetings.

You don't need a holiday to recover.

You just need rhythm.

Tiny rests build long-term endurance.

Step 6: Reflect, Don't Ruminate

After tough days, ask:

"What did I manage well?"

and

"What can I improve next time?"

Reflection builds resilience. Rumination drains it.

"Fall seven times, stand up eight."

– Japanese Proverb

Next-Level Skills

Skill in Action: Real-World Examples

Michael Jordan: Turning Failure Into Fuel

Before he became a global icon, Michael Jordan faced one of the most painful setbacks of his young life — being cut from his high school varsity basketball team. It wasn't talent he lacked — it was height and timing. Instead of breaking his confidence, the rejection became the catalyst of his legendary work ethic.

Through countless hours in the gym, relentless practice, and a mindset built on overcoming defeat, he reshaped the narrative around failure. Jordan's career would highlight that resilience is not the absence of obstacles, but the decision to rise stronger because of them.

Resilience is the choice to turn rejection into resolve.

Chapter 10: Resilience

Malcom Gladwell's Path to Mastery Through Persistence

Before Malcolm Gladwell became one of the most influential nonfiction authors of his generation, he spent years receiving rejections from magazines, struggling to find his voice as a writer. He worked as a science writer, then as a staffer at The Washington Post, where his early pieces often missed the mark. What kept him moving wasn't confidence – it was curiosity and the willingness to iterate, revise, and keep trying.

His breakthrough came only after years of experimentation. His later books, including Outliers and The Tipping Point, echo his own journey: success is rarely sudden – it is built on resilience, practice, and learning through repetition. Gladwell's story demonstrates that resilience is not loud or heroic. Sometimes it looks like simply showing up every day, long before anyone notices.

Resilience grows through repetition – long before recognition arrives.

Next-Level Skills

Bethany Hamilton: Strength After Loss

At age 13, surfer Bethany Hamilton lost her arm in a shark attack. Most would have walked away from the sport. She returned to competition within months.

Her resilience was not rooted in denial but in deep faith and determination. Through retraining her balance, re-engineering her board, and reframing her mindset, she turned loss into adaptation.

Bethany's story resonated far beyond sport. It became a testament to identity beyond circumstance – proof that resilience is not about returning to who you were but discovering who you are capable of becoming.

Resilience is recovery with reinvention.

Chapter 10: Resilience

Airbnb's Reinvention During the Pandemic

In 2020, Airbnb faced near-collapse as global travel halted overnight. Bookings dropped by 80%, and the company laid off a quarter of its staff. CEO Brian Chesky wrote an open letter acknowledging the pain while reaffirming Airbnb's mission: belonging.

Instead of retreating, the company pivoted – focusing on long-term stays and online experiences, keeping the brand alive through empathy and creativity. When travel returned, Airbnb was stronger than before. Chesky's transparent and compassionate leadership turned crisis into renewal. His decision to lead with honesty and humanity became a case study in organisational resilience.

Resilience is adaptability anchored in purpose.

Next-Level Skills

Malala Yousafzai's Courage Beyond Trauma

After being shot by the Taliban for attending school, Malala Yousafzai faced years of recovery. Yet her first question upon waking wasn't "Why me?" but "What can I do next?" She used her voice to create the Malala Fund, championing education for millions of girls worldwide.

Her resilience transcended survival – it became service. By transforming personal suffering into global advocacy, Malala proved that the most profound resilience is found in turning pain into purpose.

Resilience is when purpose becomes stronger than pain.

Resilience isn't heroic. It's human.

Chapter 10: Resilience

Weekly Reflection Exercise

Take 10 quiet minutes to reflect on these:

How do I typically respond when things don't go as planned?

What patterns help me recover from setbacks faster?

When was the last time I surprised myself with my own strength?

Who helps me regain perspective when I lose it – and how can I thank them?

Next-Level Skills

One Key Action Step This Week

When stress or difficulty arises this week, pause and ask:

"What part of this is within my control?"

Then take one small, positive action — no matter how small.

Momentum rebuilds confidence faster than perfection.

Chapter 10: Resilience

Final Reflection

Resilience isn't about never falling – it's about learning how to rise stronger each time.

It's not built in comfort, but in challenge.

It's the quiet voice that says, *"I'll try again tomorrow."*

As Maya Angelou said:

"I can be changed by what happens to me. But I refuse to be reduced by it."

Resilience turns adversity into advantage – and setbacks into stories of growth.

It's the foundation of every Next-Level you'll ever reach.

Next-Level Skills

Chapter Immediately

Resilience

WHY IT MATTERS!

- ⭐ Builds stability under stress
- ⭐ Enables faster recovery
- ⭐ Strengthens confidence
- ⭐ Inspires others
- ⭐ Supports sustained success

PRACTICAL WAYS TO BUILD THE SKILL

1. Reframe Setbacks as Setups

2. Regulate Your Energy, Not Just Your Emotions

3. Anchor to Purpose

4. Build a Support Network

5. Embrace Micro-Recovery

6. Reflect, Don't Ruminate

Chapter 10: Resilience

Take It Further ...

- *How do you define resilience in your own life?*

- *What experiences have most shaped your ability to recover and grow?*

- *How do you distinguish between healthy perseverance and burnout?*

- *What daily routines or rituals help you stay grounded?*

- *Who in your life models quiet resilience – and what do they do differently?*

- *How can you build more "micro-recovery" moments into your week?*

- *How can resilience make you not just tougher, but wiser?*

Next-Level Skills

Chapter 11: Personal Goal Setting

"Direction Over Distraction"

Next-Level Skills

Building on *Resilience*, personal goal setting is about transforming strength into strategy.

It's not about doing more – it's about doing what *matters most*.

While resilient people can withstand storms, goal-oriented people know *why* they're standing in the first place.

Clear goals give purpose to effort and meaning to momentum.

They remind you what to say *yes* to – and what to say *no* to.

Because when your direction is clear, your distractions lose power.

Chapter 11: Personal Goal Setting

"The Year That Changed Her Focus"

A mid-level manager in Brisbane used to start every year with a list of 20 goals – everything from "get fit" to "learn French" to "get promoted, for example."

By March, the list felt like a burden.

She was exhausted, busy, and unfulfilled. Each unchecked item became a quiet reminder of failure rather than motivation. She found herself scattered, making minimal progress on everything while mastering nothing.

The energy she poured into juggling so many ambitions left her drained and discouraged, questioning whether she was capable of achieving anything meaningful at all.

This year, she tried something different. She chose just three goals – one personal, one professional, and one for her well-being.

Next-Level Skills

Instead of spreading herself thin, she focused her energy like a laser. Each goal received dedicated time, attention, and resources. She broke them into manageable milestones and built systems that made progress inevitable rather than relying on willpower alone.

She tracked progress monthly and celebrated small wins.

By October, she had already achieved all three.

Not because she did more, but because she did *less – better*.

"You can do anything, but not everything."

– David Allen

Why Personal Goal Setting Matters

Goals give structure to growth.

They turn dreams into direction, and direction into discipline.

Without clear goals, effort scatters. With them, focus sharpens.

Goals act as compass points in the fog of daily demands, helping you distinguish between what's urgent and what's important. They create accountability by making the invisible visible – transforming vague aspirations into measurable milestones you can track and adjust.

When goals are well-defined, decisions become easier because you have criteria for what moves you forward and what pulls you sideways. They also provide resilience during setbacks, reminding you why you started when motivation fades.

Next-Level Skills

Here's why goal setting matters:

Personal Goal Setting
Why It Matters!

1	Creates clarity and motivation
2	Improves prioritisation
3	Builds accountability
4	Boosts confidence
5	Transforms resilience into momentum

Creates clarity and motivation

Setting personal goals gives you a clear sense of direction and purpose. You understand exactly where you're heading, which helps you to stay motivated, knowing why your efforts matter. When you have a defined target, it's easier to get started each day and to keep your energy focused on what's important.

Improves prioritisation

With well-defined goals, every decision you make can be measured against what matters most to you. This makes it much simpler to decide what to say yes or no to, reducing overwhelm and helping you spend your time and energy on tasks that truly move you forward.

Builds accountability

Goals act as a yardstick for progress, allowing you to track how far you've come and what still needs attention. By setting clear milestones, you give yourself points to check in, adjust your approach if needed, and hold yourself responsible for staying on course.

Next-Level Skills

Boosts confidence

Each milestone or small win achieved serves as evidence of your ability. As you reach these goals, your self-belief grows, giving you the courage to tackle even bigger challenges. Confidence builds with every step, making the next one that bit easier.

Transforms resilience into momentum

When setbacks happen, having clear goals gives you a reason to bounce back with renewed purpose, not just sheer persistence. Instead of feeling stuck, you recover more quickly and use each challenge as fuel to propel yourself forward, turning resilience into real momentum.

As Zig Ziglar said:

"A goal properly set is halfway reached."

Practical Ways to Build Personal Goal Setting

Goal setting is both art and structure.

The art lies in crafting goals that genuinely excite you – ones that connect to your deeper values and paint a picture of a future worth pursuing. These aren't borrowed ambitions or should-dos imposed by others. Instead, they're expressions of what matters most to you.

The structure provides the scaffolding that transforms inspiration into action: specificity that removes ambiguity, timelines that create urgency, and milestones that break intimidating mountains into climbable steps.

When art and structure work together, goals become powerful enough to pull you forward during difficult moments yet flexible enough to adapt as circumstances change. Here are six steps to make your goals inspiring – and achievable.

Next-Level Skills

Step 1: Define What Truly Matters

Start with your *why*.

Ask:

"What do I want my life and work to stand for this year?"

Align goals with values – not with trends or expectations.

Meaning fuels motivation.

Step 2: Write It Down

Unwritten goals are wishes.

When you put them on paper, they become clearer and hence, commitments.

You're more likely to achieve written goals.

Next-Level Skills

Step 3: Make Them SMARTER

Move beyond the basic SMART framework.

SMART (Specific, Measurable, Achievable, Relevant, Time-bound).

Add **E** for *Emotional* (why it matters)

and **R** for *Reviewed* (when you'll revisit it).

SMARTER goals keep you aligned *and* inspired.

Step 4: Break Big Goals Into Micro-Actions

Every big win starts with a small daily commitment.

Ask:

"What's one small action I can take this week to move closer to my goal?"

Progress builds confidence and confidence builds momentum.

Next-Level Skills

Step 5: Track Progress and Reflect Regularly

Set weekly or monthly check-ins with yourself.

Celebrate progress and recalibrate as needed.

Goals are living things – they grow as you do.

Step 6: Share Your Goals With Someone You Trust

Accountability turns intention into action.

Tell a mentor, friend, or peer.

When others know your direction, they help you stay the course.

"Discipline is the bridge between goals and accomplishment."

– Jim Rohn

Next-Level Skills

Skill in Action: Real-World Examples

Elon Musk's Vision-Driven Goals

Elon Musk is known for setting goals that sound less like business plans and more like science fiction — colonising Mars, building reusable rockets, and transforming global energy. His goals start with a question: *What would make life better for humanity?*

By framing his ambitions in service of the future, he turns impossible ideas into practical roadmaps.

At SpaceX and Tesla, his teams operate with one unifying principle — purpose before profit. Every milestone, from launch tests to electric vehicles, connects to a larger "why." Musk shows that personal goals become unstoppable when they're fuelled by mission, not metrics.

Purpose gives goals gravity.

Serena Williams and the Discipline of Micro-Goals

For Serena Williams, greatness was never one grand target – it was a thousand small, daily goals. Every training session had a purpose: improve one movement, refine one habit, strengthen one mindset. This granular focus kept her driven for over two decades at the top of tennis.

Her success reveals a truth about goal setting – progress compounds when you break ambition into action. Serena never lost sight of her long-term vision, but she built it through rituals of focus, rest, and renewal.

Big goals live inside small daily disciplines.

Next-Level Skills

Bill Gates and the Power of Measurable Impact

After leaving Microsoft, Bill Gates shifted his focus to global health through the Gates Foundation. His approach to philanthropy mirrors his approach to software: data-driven, iterative, and results-focused. Instead of vague intentions, he sets measurable goals – eradicate malaria, improve sanitation, reduce child mortality.

Gates treats every problem like a system to understand, evaluate, and improve. His success shows that clarity in measurement transforms good intentions into global outcomes.

What gets measured, gets mastered.

Chapter 11: Personal Goal Setting

Oprah Winfrey and the Vision Board of Intention

Oprah Winfrey often speaks about the power of intention – how visualising your goal makes it tangible. She keeps a vision board not as superstition, but as focus. For her, every career move – from television to film to publishing – began as a clearly visualised purpose: not *what* she wanted to achieve, but *why* she wanted it.

This alignment between intention and action fuels authenticity. Oprah teaches that setting goals isn't about chasing everything. It's about choosing what aligns with your truth, instead.

Clarity of intention turns goals into direction.

Next-Level Skills

Roger Federer's Late-Career Reinvention

In his mid-thirties, Roger Federer faced declining performance and physical strain. Instead of retiring, he reset his goals – shifting focus from domination to longevity and joy. By recalibrating his training, rest, and mindset, he achieved some of his finest seasons late in his career.

Federer's story shows that goals are not static – they evolve with identity. His adaptability in redefining success teaches that the most sustainable goals honour both ambition and balance.

Great goals evolve as you do.

Chapter 11: Personal Goal Setting

Weekly Reflection Exercise

Take 10 quiet minutes to reflect on these:

What three things matter most to me this year, and why?

Which of my goals feel meaningful, and which feel like obligations?

What daily habits can help me stay consistent with my goals?

Who can help me stay accountable and celebrate progress?

Next-Level Skills

One Key Action Step This Week

Write down *one goal* that matters deeply to you — then list *one next step* you can take within 24 hours.

Don't wait for perfect timing.

Momentum starts with one deliberate move. It is all what it takes.

Chapter 11: Personal Goal Setting

Final Reflection

Personal goal setting isn't about control – it's about direction.

It's the act of saying,

"This is what matters to me, and I'll align my actions to it."

Goals give shape to your resilience and purpose to your progress.

They help you measure growth not by busyness, but by meaning.

As Antoine de Saint-Exupéry said:

"A goal without a plan is just a wish."

When your goals align with your values, every step – even the smallest – moves you closer to the life you're meant to lead.

Next-Level Skills

Chapter Immediately

Personal Goal Setting

WHY IT MATTERS!

- ⭐ Creates clarity and motivation
- ⭐ Improves prioritisation
- ⭐ Builds accountability
- ⭐ Boosts confidence
- ⭐ Transforms resilience into momentum

PRACTICAL WAYS TO BUILD THE SKILL

1 Define What Truly Matters

2 Write It Down

3 Make Them SMARTER

4 Break Big Goals Into Micro-Actions

5 Track Progress and Reflect Regularly

6 Share Your Goals With Someone You Trust

Chapter 11: Personal Goal Setting

Take It Further ...

- What are three personal goals that would make this year truly meaningful?

- How can you connect your goals to your values and long-term vision?

- What old goals might need to be released or reframed?

- How can you measure progress without being overly perfectionist?

- Who can you share your goals with for support and accountability?

- What daily rituals keep you focused on what matters most?

- How will you celebrate progress, not just completion?

Next-Level Skills

Chapter 12: Storytelling for Influence

"Turning Insight into Impact"

Next-Level Skills

Building on *Personal Goal Setting*, storytelling for influence is where clarity meets connection.

It's how leaders turn ideas into inspiration – and information into action.

Because facts inform, but stories *transform*.

Stories don't just describe reality - they *shape* it.

They connect logic with emotion, intention with impact, and people with purpose.

The best communicators, mentors, and leaders don't just say things – they make people *feel* things.

That's storytelling for influence.

Chapter 12: Storytelling for Influence

"The Presentation That Changed Minds"

A project lead at a Sydney fintech startup had to convince senior management to invest in a new client app.

His first attempt was full of data – charts, metrics, performance graphs. It fell flat.

So, he tried again.

This time, he began with a story about a frustrated customer – a real person struggling with the current process.

He described the emotion, the delay, the impact.

Then he showed how the new app would change that story's ending.

The room went silent – and then they said "yes".

Next-Level Skills

Because he didn't just present numbers – he told a *narrative*.

He didn't just propose a solution – he created a shared vision.

"People don't buy what you do – they buy why you do it."
– Simon Sinek

Chapter 12: Storytelling for Influence

Why Storytelling for Influence Matters

In leadership, storytelling is the bridge between *intention and inspiration.*

It makes ideas memorable, visions believable, and actions meaningful.

While data appeals to logic, stories engage emotion, and its emotion that moves people to act. A well-told story creates a shared experience, allowing listeners to see themselves in the narrative and imagine their role in what comes next.

It bypasses resistance by speaking to something deeper than rational analysis – our fundamental need for meaning, connection, and purpose.

Leaders who master storytelling don't just communicate directives – they paint pictures of possibility that people want to step into.

Next-Level Skills

Here's why storytelling matters:

Storytelling for Influence
Why It Matters!

1	Builds emotional connection
2	Clarifies complex ideas
3	Drives action
4	Humanises leadership
5	Strengthens culture

Builds emotional connection

People remember how you make them feel, not just what you say. When a leader shares a story that resonates emotionally, it creates genuine connections, helping the audience to relate to both the message and the messenger on a deeper level. This sense of connection builds trust and loyalty, making the message more impactful and enduring.

Clarifies complex ideas

A story simplifies what data can't. Instead of bombarding listeners with statistics and jargon, storytelling breaks down intricate concepts into relatable scenarios, making information easier to digest and understand. Stories provide context and meaning, turning abstract ideas into something tangible and memorable.

Drives action

A well-told story makes others want to be part of the journey. By illustrating a clear vision and mapping out the path forward, stories inspire listeners to get involved and contribute. They motivate people to take action, energising teams and prompting positive change in a way that facts alone often cannot achieve.

Humanises leadership

Stories reveal authenticity, not authority. When leaders share their own experiences, challenges, and learnings, it demonstrates vulnerability and openness. This authenticity encourages others to engage and communicate honestly, fostering a culture where people feel seen and valued, rather than simply managed.

Strengthens culture

Shared stories create shared meaning. Storytelling weaves individual experiences into the fabric of an organisation's culture, helping everyone feel connected to a common purpose. These collective narratives reinforce values and traditions, build unity, and nurture a sense of belonging that is crucial for long-term success.

Chapter 12: Storytelling for Influence

As Brené Brown says:

"Maybe stories are just data with a soul."

Next-Level Skills

Practical Ways to Master Storytelling for Influence

Anyone can tell stories – but influential storytelling is intentional.

The difference between rambling anecdotes and compelling narratives lies in craft and purpose.

Influential storytellers don't just recount events – they shape them with deliberate structure, emotional arcs, and clear takeaways that serve their larger message. They know which details to include and which to strip away. They consider their audience carefully, tailoring tone, complexity, and references to resonate with specific listeners.

Most importantly, they tell stories with intention: each narrative has a job to do, whether it's building trust, illustrating a principle, inspiring action, or shifting perspective.

Here are six ways to use it powerfully.

Chapter 12: Storytelling for Influence

Step 1: Know Your Purpose

Ask yourself before speaking or writing:

"What change do I want this story to create?"

Influential stories aren't random – they're purposeful.

Next-Level Skills

Step 2: Start With Emotion, Then Add Logic

Emotion grabs attention – logic sustains it.

Lead with human experience, then support it with facts.

That balance builds credibility *and* connection.

Step 3: Keep It Simple

Clarity beats complexity.

A short, relatable story always outperforms a long, technical one.

Focus on one message – one turning point – one truth.

Next-Level Skills

Step 4: Use Real People, Real Moments

Authenticity builds influence.

Tell stories drawn from genuine experiences – your own or others'.

Audiences connect with honesty, not perfection.

Step 5: Craft a Clear Structure

Every great story has three parts:

The Setup – Introduce the challenge or context.

The Shift – Show what changed (the insight, decision, or realisation).

The Significance – Reveal why it matters now.

Simple structure, powerful delivery.

Next-Level Skills

Step 6: End With a Call to Action

The most influential stories move people towards something – reflection, empathy, or action.

Ask:

"What do I want them to think, feel, or do after hearing this?"

"Those who tell the stories rule the world."
– *Native American Proverb*

Chapter 12: Storytelling for Influence

Skill in Action: Real-World Examples

Steve Jobs and the Product Launch as Storytelling

When Steve Jobs introduced the first iPhone in 2007, he didn't just unveil a device – he told a story. He began by framing the problem, built anticipation, and revealed the solution with emotional rhythm. "Today, Apple is going to reinvent the phone," he said. The moment felt cinematic because it was carefully constructed to connect logic with feeling.

Jobs understood that influence lies not in information, but in meaning. He used narrative to turn technology into aspiration – showing that the best storytellers make the audience feel they're part of the journey.

A story turns innovation into emotion.

Next-Level Skills

Martin Luther King Jr.'s Dream of Clarity and Courage

On the steps of the Lincoln Memorial, Martin Luther King Jr. didn't deliver a policy paper – he painted a dream. Through repetition, imagery, and moral conviction, he transformed a movement into a message. His words, "I have a dream," didn't instruct – they inspired.

King's mastery lay in translating injustice into hope. He made the invisible visible through language. His storytelling reminds us that influence begins with imagination – helping people see not just what *is*, but what *could be*.

Great stories make people believe in better futures.

Chapter 12: Storytelling for Influence

Sheryl Sandberg's "Option B" — Story as Healing

After losing her husband unexpectedly, Sheryl Sandberg co-wrote *Option B*, a book that turned her grief into a universal story of resilience. By sharing her vulnerability, she gave others permission to confront their own losses. The book didn't preach strength – it demonstrated it through honesty.

Sandberg's storytelling carried both intellect and empathy, turning pain into purpose. Her courage to share what others silence made her message unforgettable: that storytelling can be a bridge between individual struggle and collective healing.

Stories that reveal truth create connection.

Next-Level Skills

Barack Obama's Narrative of Hope

Barack Obama's political rise was powered by storytelling – not slogans. His speeches wove his own journey into America's broader one, blending personal humility with national purpose. His 2008 campaign centred on a story bigger than politics: hope as a civic responsibility.

Through storytelling, Obama united diverse groups under shared ideals. His influence came not from authority but from emotional resonance. He proved that leadership begins with the story you tell – and the belief it inspires in others.

Stories unite where arguments divide.

Brené Brown's TED Talk on Vulnerability

When Brené Brown stepped on the TED stage to talk about vulnerability, she expected academic curiosity. Instead, her authenticity created a cultural movement. She blended research with humour, self-reflection, and humanity – transforming an abstract concept into an emotional revelation.

Her storytelling worked because it was real. She didn't perform vulnerability – she lived it. Brown's talk is a reminder that influence doesn't come from being perfect. It comes from being human enough to be believed.

Authenticity is the heartbeat of every great story.

Next-Level Skills

Weekly Reflection Exercise

Take 10 quiet minutes to reflect on these:

What's one story from your life or work that shaped who you are?

How can you use that story to inspire or guide others?

When you share ideas, do people remember your message — or your meaning?

What stories define your team, organisation, or culture?

Chapter 12: Storytelling for Influence

One Key Action Step This Week

Share one personal or professional story that communicates a lesson, not a lecture.

It could be in a team meeting, presentation, or even a one-on-one chat.

Focus on honesty and connection – not perfection.

The more real you are, the more relatable your story becomes.

Next-Level Skills

Final Reflection

Storytelling is how influence becomes legacy.

It's how we turn lessons into light for others to see by. Every story you tell – through words, actions, or leadership – shapes how people understand possibility.

As Maya Angelou said:

"There is no greater agony than bearing an untold story inside you."

So, tell yours.

Tell it with courage, clarity, and compassion.

Because the story you live – and the stories you share – might just be the spark that helps someone else rise.

That's what *Next-Level Leadership* truly is:
Not just achieving success – but inspiring it in others.

Chapter 12: Storytelling for Influence

Chapter Immediately

Storytelling for Influence

WHY IT MATTERS!

- ⭐ Builds emotional connection
- ⭐ Clarifies complex ideas
- ⭐ Drives action
- ⭐ Humanises leadership
- ⭐ Strengthens culture

PRACTICAL WAYS TO BUILD THE SKILL

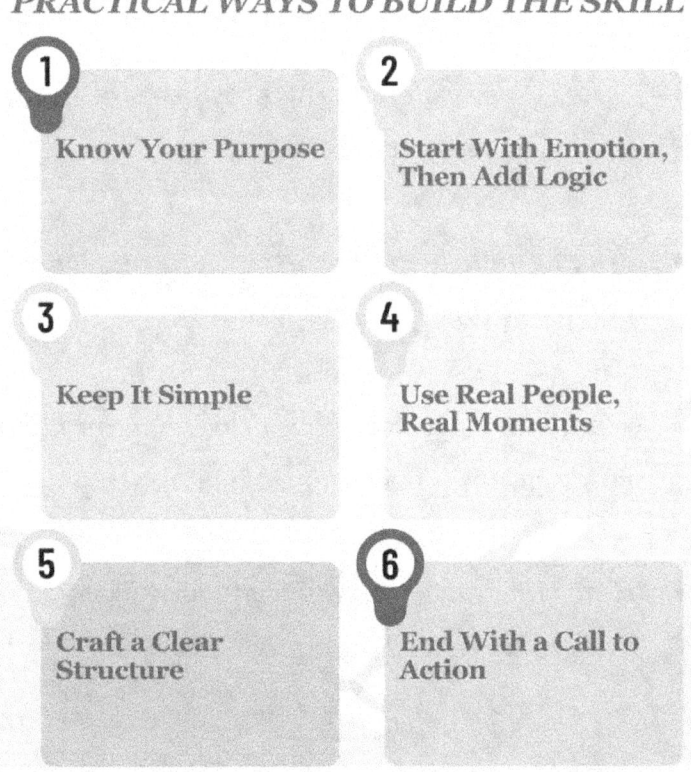

1. Know Your Purpose
2. Start With Emotion, Then Add Logic
3. Keep It Simple
4. Use Real People, Real Moments
5. Craft a Clear Structure
6. End With a Call to Action

Next-Level Skills

Take It Further ...

- *What story from your life best illustrates your values or lessons learned?*

- *How can you use storytelling to strengthen your communication and influence at work?*

- *What makes a story "stick" with you and how can you replicate that effect?*

- *How can storytelling help resolve conflict or build empathy in your team?*

- *Who in your life tells stories that move you and what do they do differently?*

- *What story are you currently living and how might you rewrite your next chapter?*

- *How can storytelling become part of your leadership toolkit going forward?*

Chapter 13: Integration – Bringing It All Together

"From Learning to Living"

Next-Level Skills

Every ending is really a beginning – the point where insight becomes practice!

Over these twelve chapters, you've explored what it means to grow – not by adding more to your plate, but by expanding **what's possible within you**.

You've learned to be self-aware and emotionally intelligent, to listen deeply, adapt confidently, think strategically, communicate clearly, resolve conflict, take ownership, lead without titles, stay resilient, set meaningful goals, and influence through stories.

Each skill, on its own, is powerful.

Together, they form a *complete way of being*.

Because *Next-Level Skills* aren't a past of some checklist – they are part of a continuum.

It's not about learning one skill after another, but weaving them together into how you think, decide, and show up every day.

Chapter 13: Integration – Bringing It All Together

"The Project of You"

A project manager once said:

"I realised the most complex project I'll ever manage is myself." And she was right.

We spend years learning how to plan, lead, and deliver – yet the real work begins when we turn those same principles inward.

When we apply curiosity to our reactions, compassion to our mistakes, and accountability to our growth – we stop *doing* leadership and start *being* leaders.

That's the quiet transformation this journey creates.

"We are what we repeatedly do. Excellence, then, is not an act but a habit."
– *Aristotle*

Next-Level Skills

The Power of Integration

Integration is the moment everything connects.

- When your *self-awareness* fuels your *emotional intelligence*.
- When *adaptability* strengthens your *strategic thinking*.
- When *clear communication* supports *conflict resolution*.
- When *accountability* amplifies *leadership without authority*.
- When *resilience* guides *goal setting*, and *storytelling* magnifies your impact.

The skills no longer live in separate boxes – they merge into one steady rhythm to your *Next-Level*.

Integration is when practice becomes instinct. When awareness becomes action.

When growth stops being a destination and becomes a *way of life*.

Chapter 13: Integration – Bringing It All Together

Leading at the Next-Level

Leadership at the Next-Level isn't about control – it's about contribution.

It's the daily decision to bring clarity where there's confusion, calm where there's chaos, and connection where there's distance.

You don't need a title to lead.
You don't need a perfect plan.
You just need the courage to keep showing up –
curious, grounded, and willing to grow.

Next-Level leaders don't have all the answers.

They ask better questions.
They listen longer.
They build others up instead of standing above them.

And in doing so, they create ripples that reach further than they'll ever see.

> *"The meaning of life is to find your gift. The purpose of life is to give it away."*
>
> – Pablo Picasso

Chapter 13: Integration – Bringing It All Together

Your Integration Practice

Here are the ways to keep your growth alive long after the last page – because reading is just the beginning, application is where transformation happens.

1. Review and Reflect

Revisit each chapter once a month or a quarter.

Pick one skill to deepen each time.

Growth compounds when reflection becomes a habit.

2. Connect the Dots

Notice how one skill supports another.

For instance, how emotional intelligence strengthens communication, or how resilience sustains accountability.

Integration lives in the spaces *between* skills.

3. Apply in Real Time

Each day, choose one skill to practice consciously – in a meeting, conversation, or decision.

Small, consistent action beats occasional intensity.

4. Teach What You Learn

The fastest way to internalise a skill is to share it.

Mentor someone, lead a workshop, or simply model what you've mastered.

Teaching turns knowledge into legacy.

5. Anchor to Purpose

Keep asking *why* you're developing these skills.

Purpose keeps growth personal.

Without it, development becomes performance.

---

6. Celebrate Progress

You don't need to reach "Next-Level" to celebrate it.

Every step forward – every pause, reflection, and realisation – *is* the Next-Level.

Next-Level Skills

Weekly Reflection Exercise

Take 10 quiet minutes to reflect on these:

Which of the twelve skills have you strengthened the most and which one needs more focus?

How do these skills show up in your daily work or relationships?

What has changed most about the way you see yourself as a leader?

What would "your Next-Level" look like six months from now?

Chapter 13: Integration – Bringing It All Together

One Key Action Step This Week

Choose one area of your life – your team, your mindset, or a specific goal – and apply *three* of the skills together.

Notice how they interact and reinforce one another.

That's integration in action.

Final Reflection

Next-Level isn't a step.

It's a ripple — made by how you think, speak, decide, and care.

You are already on your Next-Level — every time you listen with empathy, act with integrity, or choose clarity over comfort.

And as you keep integrating these skills into who you are, you'll realise something profound:

You've stopped chasing "The Next-Level."

You've become it!

"The journey doesn't end when you find your voice. It begins when you use it to lift others."
— *Unknown*

Chapter 13: Integration – Bringing It All Together

Chapter Immediately

Integration – Bringing It All Together

THE POWER OF INTEGRATION

⭐ When your self-awareness fuels your emotional intelligence.

⭐ When adaptability strengthens your strategic thinking.

⭐ When clear communication supports conflict resolution.

⭐ When accountability amplifies leadership without authority.

⭐ When resilience guides goal setting, and storytelling magnifies your impact.

LEADING AT THE NEXT-LEVEL

Next-Level leaders don't have all the answers.

They ask better questions.

They listen longer.

They build others up instead of standing above them.

YOUR INTEGRATION PRACTICE

Celebrate Progress
Every step forward – every pause, reflection, and realisation – is the Next-Level.

Review and Reflect
Growth compounds when reflection becomes a habit.

Anchor to Purpose
Without it, development becomes performance.

Connect the Dots
Integration lives in the spaces between skills.

Teach What You Learn
Teaching turns knowledge into legacy.

Apply in Real Time
Small, consistent action beats occasional intensity.

Next-Level Skills

Take It Further ...

- *What does "integration" mean to you in your own life and leadership?*

- *How will you continue practising these skills beyond this book?*

- *Who can you share this journey with — to grow together?*

- *What daily rituals can help you stay grounded and self-aware?*

- *How can you make reflection a regular part of your work and leadership rhythm?*

- *What impact do you most want to leave, and which skills will get you there?*

Epilogue – The Journey Continues

Every project has a completion date.

But growth doesn't.

You've explored twelve skills – and then learned how to integrate them into one cohesive mindset.

Yet the real journey begins *after* this book ends.

Because *Next-Level Skills* isn't about mastering a list – it's about embodying a way of living and leading.

It's about bringing self-awareness to every meeting, empathy to every challenge, and purpose to every decision.

If there's one message to carry forward, it's this: you already have what it takes to lead, connect, and create impact.

Next-Level Skills

This book simply helped you name it, nurture it, and navigate it.

Keep refining your awareness.

Keep strengthening your adaptability.

Keep choosing clarity over comfort.

And whenever the path feels uncertain, come back to where it all began – the quiet moment of reflection where growth starts again.

Because every Next-Level begins with a single conscious choice.

Next Steps – Putting It into Practice

Growth is not a one-time event. It's a rhythm – a blend of reflection, experimentation, and renewal.

The insights you've gained and the skills you've explored in this book are merely seeds.

Without tending, they'll remain dormant potential rather than flourishing practice.

Real transformation happens not in the moment of understanding but in the weeks and months that follow, when you deliberately integrate new behaviours into your daily life.

This requires building systems that support continuous learning – routines for reflection that help you extract lessons from your on-going experience, practices for experimentation that let you test and

Next-Level Skills

refine new approaches, and rituals for renewal that prevent burnout and keep curiosity alive.

The leaders who evolve consistently aren't necessarily the most talented. However, they're the ones who've mastered the art of sustained practice, turning sporadic bursts of motivation into steady habits of growth.

What follows are practical strategies to ensure this book becomes a catalyst for lasting change rather than a fleeting inspiration.

1. Focus on One Skill at a Time

Revisit one of the twelve skills weekly or fortnightly or monthly, whichever suits you and your pace!

Read your notes, reflect on progress, and set a micro-goal to apply it at work or in life.

By end, you'll have cycled through all twelve with deeper mastery.

---

2. Build Your "Next-Level Journal"

Use a journal to capture reflections, key lessons, and real-world applications. At the end of each rhythm cycle, ask:

- *What skill did I practise most?*
- *What situation challenged me?*
- *What did I learn about myself or others?*

3. Form a Growth Circle

Invite colleagues or friends to read selected chapters together.

Share insights, discuss challenges, and hold each other accountable for practising one skill each week.

Growth shared is growth sustained.

---

4. Teach, Mentor, and Model

Nothing reinforces learning like teaching it.
Share the "Next-Level Skills" framework in your team meetings, mentoring sessions, or leadership workshops.

Lead by demonstration, not declaration.

5. Stay Curious

Read widely. Listen deeply. Ask better questions.

Curiosity is the engine that keeps growth alive.

"Once you stop learning, you start declining."
– Albert Einstein

---

6. Redefine the 'Next-Level' Often

Your definition of success will evolve – and that's the whole point!

Every time you reach a new level of clarity or competence, ask yourself:

"What does my Next-Level look like now?"

Next-Level Skills

Book Immediately

Each chapter has its own *"Chapter Immediately"* segment, designed to give you a rapid overview of actionable ideas and frameworks specific to that topic.

This section serves as a concise roundup of all the *"Chapter Immediately"* highlights from each chapter.

Here, you'll find quick-reference points collated from all 12 chapters. Each chapter is focused on a distinct development skill to take you to your *Next-Level*.

This compilation provides you with all the essential tools and prompts from the entire book in a single, accessible resource, thereby supporting you're your continued learning and practical implementation.

Whether you are preparing for a meeting, mentoring colleagues, or seeking to refresh your knowledge, this section can help you with quick reference and application of key insights.

Next-Level Skills

Part I
The Inner Foundation: Mastering Self
Growth begins within

CHAPTER 1	CHAPTER 2	CHAPTER 3
Self-Awareness	**Emotional Intelligence**	**Active Listening**
The Foundation Of Every Next-Level Skill	*The Skill That Amplifies Every Other One*	*The Hidden Power Behind Every Great Conversation*

Part II
The Adaptive Mindset: Thriving in Change
Flexibility is the modern superpower

CHAPTER 4	CHAPTER 5	CHAPTER 6
Adaptability	**Strategic Thinking**	**Clear Communication**
The Art of Staying Steady When Everything Changes	*Seeing the Forest and the Trees*	*Turning Vision into Understanding*

Part III
The Human Connection: Building Trust and Collaboration
Relationships are the real currency of leadership

CHAPTER 7	CHAPTER 8	CHAPTER 9
Conflict Resolution	**Accountability**	**Leadership Without Authority**
Turning Friction into Forward Motion	*Owning the Outcome – Not Just the Effort*	*Influence Without a Title*

Part IV
The Growth Continuum: Sustaining Purpose and Impact
True growth is built on resilience, clarity, and meaning

CHAPTER 10	CHAPTER 11	CHAPTER 12
Resilience	**Personal Goal Setting**	**Storytelling for Influence**
Bending Without Breaking	*Direction Over Distraction*	*Turning Insight into Impact*

CHAPTER 13
Integration – Bringing It All Together

From Learning to Living

Book Immediately

#1: Self-Awareness

Self-Awareness

WHY IT MATTERS!

- ⭐ Improves Emotional Intelligence
- ⭐ Strengthens Relationships
- ⭐ Enhances Decision-Making
- ⭐ Boosts Leadership Effectiveness
- ⭐ Encourages Personal Growth

PRACTICAL WAYS TO BUILD THE SKILL

1. Write Your Personal "User Manual"
2. Seek Real Feedback (Without Defending It)
3. Pause Before You React
4. Audit Your Energy
5. Clarify Your Core Values
6. Schedule Reflection Time Like a Meeting (with Yourself!)

Next-Level Skills

#2: *Emotional Intelligence*

Emotional Intelligence

WHY IT MATTERS!

- ⭐ Improves communication and collaboration
- ⭐ Reduces stress and conflict
- ⭐ Strengthens leadership presence
- ⭐ Enhances resilience
- ⭐ Inspires loyalty

PRACTICAL WAYS TO BUILD THE SKILL

1 Name What You Feel

2 Observe Before You Respond

3 Read the Room

4 Practice Empathic Curiosity

5 Regulate Before You Communicate

6 Lead with Emotional Transparency

#3: Active Listening

Active Listening

WHY IT MATTERS!

- ★ Builds trust and rapport
- ★ Reduces misunderstandings
- ★ Enhances influence
- ★ Improves problem-solving
- ★ Boosts leadership presence

PRACTICAL WAYS TO BUILD THE SKILL

1. Be Fully Present

2. Listen to Understand, Not to Reply

3. Reflect and Paraphrase

4. Read the Unsaid

5. Ask Clarifying Questions

6. Respond with Empathy and Intention

Next-Level Skills

#4: Adaptability

Adaptability

WHY IT MATTERS!

- ⭐ Drives innovation
- ⭐ Reduces stress
- ⭐ Improves problem-solving
- ⭐ Builds resilience
- ⭐ Elevates leadership

PRACTICAL WAYS TO BUILD THE SKILL

1 Reframe Uncertainty as Information

2 Practice Micro-Flexibility

3 Stay Curious, Not Certain

4 Learn Fast, Fail Smart

5 Regulate Emotion Before Reaction

6 Embrace Continuous Reinvention

#5: Strategic Thinking

Strategic Thinking

WHY IT MATTERS!

- ⭐ Creates direction amid uncertainty
- ⭐ Turns chaos into clarity
- ⭐ Builds long-term influence
- ⭐ Drives innovation
- ⭐ Prevents burnout

PRACTICAL WAYS TO BUILD THE SKILL

1. Ask "What's the Bigger Picture?"
2. Think in Horizons
3. Connect the Dots
4. Scenario-Map Your Decisions
5. Create Thinking Space
6. Simplify to Amplify

Next-Level Skills

#6: Clear Communication

Clear Communication

WHY IT MATTERS!

- ⭐ Saves time and reduces rework
- ⭐ Strengthens credibility
- ⭐ Improves relationships
- ⭐ Enhances decision-making
- ⭐ Drives accountability

PRACTICAL WAYS TO BUILD THE SKILL

1. Know Your Message

2. Simplify Your Language

3. Structure Before You Speak

4. Check for Understanding

5. Match Words with Tone and Body Language

6. Communicate with Empathy

#7: Conflict Resolution

Conflict Resolution

WHY IT MATTERS!

- ⭐ Builds trust through transparency
- ⭐ Encourages innovation
- ⭐ Reduces workplace stress
- ⭐ Improves decision quality
- ⭐ Strengthens leadership credibility

PRACTICAL WAYS TO BUILD THE SKILL

1 Redefine Conflict

2 Separate People from Problems

3 Listen to Understand Before Responding

4 Identify Shared Goals

5 Manage Emotions, Not Just Arguments

6 Follow Up After Resolution

Next-Level Skills

#8: Accountability

Accountability

WHY IT MATTERS!
- ⭐ Builds reliability and credibility
- ⭐ Creates clarity
- ⭐ Drives performance
- ⭐ Encourages learning
- ⭐ Strengthens culture

PRACTICAL WAYS TO BUILD THE SKILL

1. Define Clear Expectations
2. Set Measurable Outcomes
3. Model It Yourself
4. Create Check-Ins, Not Check-Ups
5. Address Gaps Early
6. Celebrate Ownership

#9: Leadership Without Authority

Leadership Without Authority

WHY IT MATTERS!

- ★ Empowers everyone
- ★ Builds trust and collaboration
- ★ Encourages innovation
- ★ Develops future leaders
- ★ Creates resilience

PRACTICAL WAYS TO BUILD THE SKILL

1. Build Trust Through Reliability
2. Master the Art of Listening
3. Influence Through Expertise
4. Elevate Others
5. Communicate with Confidence and Respect
6. Model the Behaviours You Want to See

Next-Level Skills

#10: Resilience

Resilience

WHY IT MATTERS!

- ⭐ Builds stability under stress
- ⭐ Enables faster recovery
- ⭐ Strengthens confidence
- ⭐ Inspires others
- ⭐ Supports sustained success

PRACTICAL WAYS TO BUILD THE SKILL

1. Reframe Setbacks as Setups

2. Regulate Your Energy, Not Just Your Emotions

3. Anchor to Purpose

4. Build a Support Network

5. Embrace Micro-Recovery

6. Reflect, Don't Ruminate

#11: Personal Goal Setting

Personal Goal Setting

WHY IT MATTERS!

- ⭐ Creates clarity and motivation
- ⭐ Improves prioritisation
- ⭐ Builds accountability
- ⭐ Boosts confidence
- ⭐ Transforms resilience into momentum

PRACTICAL WAYS TO BUILD THE SKILL

1. Define What Truly Matters

2. Write It Down

3. Make Them SMARTER

4. Break Big Goals Into Micro-Actions

5. Track Progress and Reflect Regularly

6. Share Your Goals With Someone You Trust

Next-Level Skills

#12: Storytelling for Influence

Storytelling for Influence

WHY IT MATTERS!

- ⭐ Builds emotional connection
- ⭐ Clarifies complex ideas
- ⭐ Drives action
- ⭐ Humanises leadership
- ⭐ Strengthens culture

PRACTICAL WAYS TO BUILD THE SKILL

1. Know Your Purpose

2. Start With Emotion, Then Add Logic

3. Keep It Simple

4. Use Real People, Real Moments

5. Craft a Clear Structure

6. End With a Call to Action

Book Immediately

#13: Integration

Integration – Bringing It All Together

THE POWER OF INTEGRATION

⭐ When your self-awareness fuels your emotional intelligence.

⭐ When adaptability strengthens your strategic thinking.

⭐ When clear communication supports conflict resolution.

⭐ When accountability amplifies leadership without authority.

⭐ When resilience guides goal setting, and storytelling magnifies your impact.

LEADING AT THE NEXT-LEVEL

Next-Level leaders don't have all the answers.

They ask better questions.

They listen longer.

They build others up instead of standing above them.

YOUR INTEGRATION PRACTICE

Celebrate Progress
Every step forward – every pause, reflection, and realisation – is the Next-Level.

Review and Reflect
Growth compounds when reflection becomes a habit.

Anchor to Purpose
Without it, development becomes performance.

Connect the Dots
Integration lives in the spaces between skills.

Teach What You Learn
Teaching turns knowledge into legacy.

Apply in Real Time
Small, consistent action beats occasional intensity.

Next-Level Skills

Appendix I – Tools and Practices

Here are a few practical frameworks and reflection prompts from throughout the book, consolidated for easy use.

The Reflection Framework (from Chapter 1 & 13)

After any experience, ask:
1. What happened?
2. What did I feel or think?
3. What did I learn?
4. What will I do differently next time?

Next-Level Skills

The 6-Step Goal Alignment (from Chapter 11)

1. Define your *why*.
2. Write it down.
3. Make it SMARTER.
4. Break it down.
5. Track and reflect.
6. Celebrate and adjust.

The Influence Equation (from Chapter 12)

Emotion + Clarity + Purpose = Impact.

Use emotion to connect, clarity to communicate, and purpose to inspire action.

The Resilience Reset (from Chapter 10)

When under stress, pause and ask:

- *What's in my control?*
- *What's one small step forward?*
- *What does progress look like today?*

The Accountability Compass (from Chapter 8)

Own, Act, Reflect, Repeat.

Accountability isn't a destination – it's a rhythm.

Next-Level Skills

Appendix II – Next-Level Skills Planner

> *"What gets written gets remembered. What gets measured gets mastered."*

Growth doesn't happen by accident – it happens by design.

This planner helps you *intentionally* practise and track your progress across the twelve core skills.

You can use it **weekly or fortnightly or monthly**, depending on your rhythm.

It's structured to balance reflection, action, and accountability – so you can see and celebrate your growth in real time.

Next-Level Skills

Step 1: Choose Your Focus Skill

Each week (or fortnight or month), pick one of the twelve *Next-Level Skills* to focus on.

Next-Level Skill	Brief Focus	Why It Matters to You
Self-Awareness	Understanding your patterns	
Emotional Intelligence	Managing emotions effectively	
Active Listening	Deepening connection and trust	
Adaptability	Thriving through change	
Strategic Thinking	Seeing the big picture	
Clear Communication	Expressing with clarity and confidence	

Appendix II – Next-Level Skills Planner

Next-Level Skill	Brief Focus	Why It Matters to You
Conflict Resolution	Turning tension into trust	
Accountability	Owning actions and outcomes	
Leadership Without Authority	Influencing through integrity	
Resilience	Staying steady under stress	
Personal Goal Setting	Aligning direction with purpose	
Storytelling for Influence	Inspiring through meaning	

💡 *Tip:* Start with one skill that feels most relevant right now. Growth flows best from what's real, not what's ideal.

Next-Level Skills

Step 2: Define Your Intentions

Use this section at the start of each period.

Focus Skill: _____

Why This Matters to Me Now:

_____

What Success Looks Like:

_____

Appendix II – Next-Level Skills Planner

Step 3: Set Micro-Actions

Growth happens through small, deliberate steps.

Action	When	How Will I Measure It?
Example: Pause before reacting in tense meetings	Daily	Track emotional tone afterward

Next-Level Skills

Step 4: Reflection Prompts

At the end of each cycle, take 10 quiet minutes to reflect.

1. What did I practise well this period?

_____
_____
_____

2. What challenged me the most?

_____
_____
_____

3. What did I learn about myself?

_____
_____
_____

Appendix II – Next-Level Skills Planner

4. How did this skill affect my interactions or decisions?

_____
_____
_____

5. What's one thing I'll continue or change next week?

_____
_____
_____
_____

Next-Level Skills

Step 5: Progress Tracker

Use this quick tracker to measure how consistently you applied your focus skill.
You can use a 1–5 scale (1 = Rarely, 5 = Consistently).

Day/Week	Focus Skill	Confidence (1–5)	Key Win	Key Lesson
1				
2				
3				
4				
5				
6				
7				

At the end of each cycle, average your confidence rating – and celebrate progress, not perfection.

Appendix II – Next-Level Skills Planner

Step 6: Integration Reflection (Monthly Summary)

At the end of each month (or after every 4-week cycle), use this page to connect your learnings.

1. Which skills did I practise most?

_____

_____

2. What patterns or themes emerged across weeks?

_____

_____

3. Where did I notice growth – internally and externally?

_____

_____

4. Which skill will I focus on next? Why?

_____

_____

5. How do these learnings connect to my broader goals?

_____

_____

Next-Level Skills

Optional: Team or Mentorship Version

If you're using this planner in a **team or coaching setting**, add a short check-in:

Reflection Prompt	My Response	Partner's/Coach's Feedback
What's one area of visible improvement this week?		
What skill would I like support on next?		
What am I most proud of?		

Final Note

This planner is not a scorecard.

It's a *mirror* – reflecting how intentionally you're showing up at your decided pace – each week, each fortnight, each month.

Use it as a living document: scribble, rewrite, adjust, repeat.

Growth isn't linear – it's layered, like leadership itself.

And remember:

"Consistency beats intensity when it comes to growth."

So, choose your pace, either weekly or fortnightly or monthly and keep moving forward, one conscious skill at a time.

Next-Level Skills

Looking Ahead Together!

This book was never meant to end at Chapter 13.

It was meant to begin a new one – **yours!**

Because *Next-Level Skills* aren't a destination.

They serve a direction.

It's the choice, every day, to bring order to chaos, clarity to communication, and purpose to progress.

And if you've read this far – you've already started.

Next-Level Skills

Thank you for taking this journey – not just through these pages, but through yourself.

The world doesn't need more leaders with authority. It needs more leaders with *authenticity*.

As you go forward, remember:

Leadership is not about perfection – it's about presence.

And your presence, when rooted in clarity, empathy, and courage, is already *Next-Level*.

Keep Going, Keep Growing!

About the Author

Abhishek Sharma

Author, Mentor, Coach, Technology Leader

Abhishek Sharma is a seasoned professional and mentor with over two decades of experience leading large-scale projects, digital transformations, and change initiatives.

Abhishek has collaborated with diverse teams across industries and continents.

His approach to leadership blends strategy with humanity – balancing precision in execution with empathy in communication.

Beyond professional life, Abhishek is enthusiastic about developing the *human side of leadership.*

Next-Level Skills

Through his **Next-Level Skills** newsletter and workshops, he helps professionals build practical skills in self-awareness, emotional intelligence, adaptability, and influence – the qualities that turn managers into leaders.

He believes that growth is not about hierarchy but about habit, not about titles but about transformation.

When he's not coaching or leading projects, Abhishek enjoys writing, mentoring emerging leaders, and exploring how AI, psychology, and purpose intersect in the future of work.

"Reinventing yourself is not about changing who you are but about uncovering the potential you've always had and daring to shape it for tomorrow."

References

Below is the consolidated list of all quotes, thinkers, and sources referenced throughout **Next-Level Skills** – Chapters 1 to 13:

General Inspiration

- **Stephen R. Covey** – The 7 Habits of Highly Effective People
- **Daniel Goleman** – Working with Emotional Intelligence
- **Brené Brown** – Dare to Lead
- **Simon Sinek** – Start with Why
- **John C. Maxwell** – The 21 Irrefutable Laws of Leadership
- **Viktor E. Frankl** – Man's Search for Meaning
- **Jim Rohn** – The Art of Exceptional Living
- **Robin Sharma** – The Leader Who Had No Title

> Next-Level Skills

- **Carol Dweck** – Mindset: The New Psychology of Success
- **Adam Grant** – Think Again
- **Charles Duhigg** – The Power of Habit
- **Angela Duckworth** – Grit
- **James Clear** – Atomic Habits

Quotes Referenced in the Book

Aristotle – "Knowing yourself is the beginning of all wisdom."

Daniel Goleman – "If your emotional abilities aren't in hand, no matter how smart you are, you're not going to get very far."

Stephen R. Covey – "Accountability breeds response-ability."

Brené Brown – "Daring leaders must care for people and hold them accountable for their behaviours."

References

Albert Einstein – "If you can't explain it simply, you don't understand it well enough."

Leonardo da Vinci – "Simplicity is the ultimate sophistication."

John C. Maxwell – "Leadership is influence – nothing more, nothing less."

Courtney Lynch – "Leaders inspire accountability through their ability to accept responsibility before they place blame."

Maya Angelou – "I can be changed by what happens to me. But I refuse to be reduced by it."

Pablo Picasso – "The meaning of life is to find your gift. The purpose of life is to give it away."

Dieter F. Uchtdorf – "It's your reaction to adversity, not adversity itself, that determines how your life's story will develop."

Zig Ziglar – "A goal properly set is halfway reached."

Next-Level Skills

Jim Rohn – "Discipline is the bridge between goals and accomplishment."

Viktor Frankl – "When we are no longer able to change a situation, we are challenged to change ourselves."

Robin Sharma – "You don't need a title to be a leader."

Albert Schweitzer – "Example is leadership."

Native American Proverb – "Those who tell the stories rule the world."

Simon Sinek – "People don't buy what you do – they buy why you do it."

David Allen – "You can do anything, but not everything."

Antoine de Saint-Exupéry – "A goal without a plan is just a wish."

References

Japanese Proverb – "Fall seven times, stand up eight."

Unknown – "The journey doesn't end when you find your voice. It begins when you use it to lift others."

Real-World Examples & Sources

Chapter 1 – Self-Awareness

- Gallo, C. (2017, September 26). *Microsoft CEO Satya Nadella: Empathy makes you a better innovator*. Forbes. https://www.forbes.com/sites/carminegallo/2017/09/26/microsoft-ceo-satya-nadella-empathy-makes-you-a-better-innovator/
- Nadella, S., Shaw, G., & Nichols, J. (2017). *Hit Refresh: The Quest to Rediscover Microsoft's Soul and Imagine a Better Future for Everyone*. Harper Business.
- Swedish Wealth Institute. (n.d.). *The success habits of Oprah Winfrey: A personal development guide*.

- https://swedishwealthinstitute.com/oprah-winfrey/the-success-habits-of-oprah-winfrey-a-personal-development-guide/
- Winfrey, O. (2020). *The path made clear: Discovering your life's direction and purpose.* Flatiron Books.
- Dalio, R. (2017). *Principles: Life and Work.* Simon & Schuster.
- Harvard Business Review. (2019, October 1). *Radical transparency can reduce bias – but only if it's done right.* https://hbr.org/2019/10/radical-transparency-can-reduce-bias-but-only-if-its-done-right
- ESPN. (2016, September 8). *Serena Williams US Open post-match interview.* ASAP Sports. http://www.asapsports.com/show_interview.php?id=123199
- ESPN. (2021, August 27). *Serena Williams reflects on motherhood and tennis.* https://www.espn.com/tennis/story/_/id/32093645/serena-williams-reflects-motherhood-tennis
- Colvin, G. (2010, November 11). *Starbucks: Schultz needs to get real.* Fortune.

https://fortune.com/2008/11/11/starbucks-schultz-needs-to-get-real/
- MBA Knowledge Base. (n.d.). *Case study: Starbucks' resilient turnaround under Howard Schultz in 2008.* https://www.mbaknol.com/management-case-studies/case-study-starbucks-resilient-turnaround-under-howard-schultz-in-2008/

Chapter 2 – Emotional Intelligence

- Brackett, M. A., Rivers, S. E., & Salovey, P. (2011). Emotional intelligence: Implications for personal, social, academic, and workplace success. Social and Personality Psychology Compass, 5(1), 88-103.
- Goleman, D. (1998). Working with emotional intelligence. New York: Bantam Books.
- Salovey, P., & Mayer, J. D. (1990). Emotional intelligence. Imagination, Cognition and Personality, 9(3), 185-211.
- Nagesh, A. (2019, March 21). *Jacinda Ardern: A leader with love on full display.* BBC News.

https://www.bbc.co.uk/news/world-asia-47630129
- She Rises Studios. (2023, April 25). *Leading with empathy: Jacinda Ardern's legacy of compassionate leadership.* https://www.sherisesstudios.com/post/leading-with-empathy-jacinda-ardern-s-legacy-of-compassionate-leadership
- Khorana, S. (2023). *Jacinda Ardern and the politics of leadership empathy: Towards emotional communities of transformation.* In S. Khorana (Ed.), Mediated emotions of migration (pp. 32–44). Cambridge University Press. https://www.cambridge.org/core/books/mediated-emotions-of-migration/jacinda-ardern-and-the-politics-of-leadership-empathy-towards-emotional-communities-of-transformation/904B8E67ACB844BA64AF68E854ED76A4
- Nadella, S., Shaw, G., & Nichols, J. (2017). *Hit refresh: The quest to rediscover Microsoft's soul and imagine a better future for everyone.* Harper Business.

References

- Harvard Business Review. (2021, October 27). *Microsoft's Satya Nadella on flexible work, the metaverse, and the power of empathy.* https://hbr.org/2021/10/microsofts-satya-nadella-on-flexible-work-the-metaverse-and-the-power-of-empathy
- Inspire & Rise. (n.d.). *How Satya Nadella transformed Microsoft with empathy and innovation.* https://www.inspireandrise.com/satya-nadellas-empathetic-innovation-at-microsoft/
- Obama, M. (2018). *Becoming.* Crown Publishing Group.
- Canfield, D. (2018, November 12). *Michelle Obama's Becoming review: An honest, sharp memoir.* Entertainment Weekly. https://ew.com/books/2018/11/12/michelle-obama-becoming-review/
- Shand-Baptiste, K. (2018, November 16). *Becoming by Michelle Obama, review: An honest endeavour.* The Independent. https://www.independent.co.uk/arts-entertainment/books/reviews/becoming-

- michelle-obama-review-book-memoir-barack-first-lady-a8634301.html
- Penguin Books Australia. (n.d.). *Becoming by Michelle Obama.* https://www.penguin.com.au/books/becoming-9780241982976
- Reisinger, D. (2020, July 25). *CEOs need to learn Tim Cook's empathy rule of management.* Inc. https://www.inc.com/don-reisinger/ceos-need-to-learn-tim-cooks-empathy-rule-of-management.html
- UMA Technology. (2025, February 25). *How Apple has changed under new CEO Tim Cook.* https://umatechnology.org/how-apple-has-changed-under-new-ceo-tim-cook/
- Gomes, G. (2025, January 8). *What can modern leaders take from Tim Cook's leadership style?* CTO Magazine. https://ctomagazine.com/leadership-takeaways-from-apple-ceo-tim-coo/
- Winch, G. (2014, October 11). *What Malala Yousafzai teaches us about psychological health.* Psychology Today. https://www.psychologytoday.com/intl/blog/t

References

he-squeaky-wheel/201410/what-malala-yousafzai-teaches-us-about-psychological-health
- NobelPrize.org. (2014). *Malala Yousafzai – Speed read.* https://www.nobelprize.org/prizes/peace/2014/yousafzai/speedread/

Chapter 3 – Active Listening

- Mandela, N. (1994). *Long walk to freedom: The autobiography of Nelson Mandela*. Little, Brown and Company.
- Warnasuriya, W. (2023, April 8). *Lessons in leadership: A summary of Nelson Mandela's "Long Walk to Freedom"*. LinkedIn. https://www.linkedin.com/pulse/lessons-leadership-summary-nelson-mandelas-long-walk-wasantha
- Read, J. H. (2010). *Leadership and power in Nelson Mandela's Long Walk to Freedom*. College of Saint Benedict/Saint John's University.

- https://digitalcommons.csbsju.edu/polsci_pubs/5/
- Wojnicki, A. (2024, April 18). *The most valuable and underrated leadership skill? Listening.* Inc. https://www.inc.com/andrea-wojnicki/the-most-valuable-under-rated-leadership-skill-listening.html
- Global Coach Group. (n.d.). *Indra Nooyi's quiet leadership that transformed PepsiCo.* https://globalcoachgroup.com/indra-nooyis-quiet-leadership-that-transformed-pepsico/
- Lay, J., & Coates, T. (2017, April 10). *Barack Obama is okay with the criticism.* The Atlantic. https://www.theatlantic.com/video/index/522486/barack-obama-on-criticism-and-fervor/
- Buncombe, A. (2017, December 29). *Barack Obama shares stories to counter the 'bad news' of 2017.* The Independent. https://www.independent.co.uk/news/world/americas/us-politics/obama-is-sharing-his-favourite-stories-of-2017-to-counter-the-years-bad-news-a8133716.html
- Muller, J. (2015, January 14). *What Mary Barra's growth strategy says about the new*

GM. Forbes. https://www.forbes.com/sites/joannmuller/2015/01/14/what-mary-barras-growth-strategy-says-about-the-new-gm/

- Wikipedia contributors. (2024). *Mary Barra*. Wikipedia. https://en.wikipedia.org/wiki/Mary_Barra
- News Bharati. (2020, January 6). *Knowledge is gained only by listening, contemplating and then practicing, says Dalai Lama*. https://www.newsbharati.com/Encyc/2020/1/6/dalai-lama-in-bodhgaya-.html
- Snibbe, S. (2020, July 7). *The Dalai Lama's "simple meditation" from Ten Percent Happier*. A Skeptic's Path to Enlightenment. https://www.skepticspath.org/blog/dalai-lama-simple-meditation-ten-percent-happier-dan-harris/
- Center for Healthy Minds. (2020, October 9). *Change your mind, change the world: A recorded dialogue with His Holiness the Dalai Lama*. https://centerhealthyminds.org/news/events/change-your-mind-change-the-world-a-

recorded-dialogue-with-his-holiness-the-dalai-lama-the-world-we-make-2020

Chapter 4 – Adaptability

- Brennan, L. (2018, October 12). *How Netflix expanded to 190 countries in 7 years*. Harvard Business Review. https://hbr.org/2018/10/how-netflix-expanded-to-190-countries-in-7-years
- Moscoso, P., Lago, A., & Sastre Boquet, I. (2021, February 7). *Netflix: From DVD-by-Mail to Streaming* [Case study]. Harvard Business Publishing. https://hbsp.harvard.edu/product/IES822-PDF-ENG
- Toyota Industries Corporation. (2017). *Kaizen (Improvement) Activities across Diverse Business Domains* [PDF report]. Toyota Industries Report 2017. https://www.toyota-industries.com/investors/items/TICOReport2017_E_p28-31_special_feature2.pdf
- Toyota Motor Corporation. (n.d.). *Toyota Kaizen Movement Program*. Toyota Global

References

Site. https://www.toyota-global.com/sustainability/social_contribution/vision/smiles/toyota-kaizen-movement/

- Lanyon, C. (2016, November 14). *Years of rejection just made J.K. Rowling more determined.* New York Magazine. https://nymag.com/vindicated/2016/11/years-of-rejection-just-made-j-k-rowling-more-determined.html

- The Guardian. (2016, March 25). *J.K. Rowling posts letters of rejection on Twitter.* https://www.theguardian.com/books/2016/mar/25/jk-rowling-harry-potter-posts-letters-of-rejection-on-twitter

- Mohon, L. (2020, April 6). *Apollo 13: The successful failure.* NASA. https://www.nasa.gov/missions/apollo/apollo-13-the-successful-failure/

- NASA. (2011, September 30). *Failure is not an option.* NASA Image Article. https://www.nasa.gov/image-article/failure-not-an-option/

- ESPN. (2019, May 27). *French Open 2019 – Serena Williams fights through sluggish start*

to win opener. https://www.espn.com/tennis/story/_/id/26833144/french-open-2019-serena-williams-fights-sluggish-start-win-opener
- Garber, G. (2012, August 14). *Tennis – Williams' reinvention is almost perfection.* ESPN. https://www.espn.com.au/tennis/story/_/id/8267699/tennis-williams-reinvention-almost-perfection

Chapter 5 – Strategic Thinking

- Jobs, S. (2005, June 12). *Stanford University Commencement Address.* Stanford University. https://news.stanford.edu/2005/06/14/jobs-061505/
- Rev. (n.d.). *Steve Jobs Stanford Commencement Speech Transcript (2005).* https://www.rev.com/transcripts/steve-jobs-stanford-commencement-speech-transcript-2005
- Amazon. (1997). *Amazon's Original 1997 Letter to Shareholders.*

References

- https://www.aboutamazon.com/news/company-news/amazons-original-1997-letter-to-shareholders
- Botticello, C. (n.d.). *Read All of Amazon's Shareholder Letters From 1997–2018*. Medium. https://readmedium.com/read-all-of-amazons-shareholder-letters-from-1997-2018-a9cec14d947c
- Sheetz, M. (2021, April 23). *Elon Musk aiming for Mars so humanity is not a single-planet species*. CNBC. https://www.cnbc.com/2021/04/23/elon-musk-aiming-for-mars-so-humanity-is-not-a-single-planet-species.html
- Pereira, D. (2025, March 17). *SpaceX Mission and Vision Statement*. Business Model Analyst. https://businessmodelanalyst.com/spacex-mission-and-vision-statement/
- Sandberg, S., & Grant, A. (2017). *Option B: Facing adversity, building resilience, and finding joy*. Knopf.
- Penguin Books Australia. (n.d.). *Option B by Sheryl Sandberg*.

- https://www.penguin.com.au/books/option-b-9780753548295
- Churchill Archive Centre. (n.d.). *Churchill as Strategist in World War Two*. https://www.churchillarchive.com/churchill-as-strategist-in-world-war-two
- Packwood, A., & Roberts, S. (n.d.). *How Churchill Waged War*. University of Cambridge. https://www.cam.ac.uk/stories/churchill-at-war
- Taylor, J. (n.d.). *How Churchill Led Britain to Victory in World War 2*. Imperial War Museums. https://www.iwm.org.uk/history/how-churchill-led-britain-to-victory-in-the-second-world-war

Chapter 6 – Clear Communication

- Gallo, C. (2017). *Barack Obama: A master class in public speaking* [PDF]. Speakizy. http://speakizy.lu/wp-content/uploads/2017/04/Barack-Obama-A-Master-Class-in-Public-Speaking.pdf

- Elliott, A. (2017, February 6). *A brief analysis of Barack Obama's speaking style*. LinkedIn. https://www.linkedin.com/pulse/brief-analysis-barack-obamas-speaking-style-aidan-elliott

- Brown, B. (2010, June). *The power of vulnerability* [TED Talk]. TEDxHouston. https://www.ted.com/talks/brene_brown_the_power_of_vulnerability

- Brown, B. (2010, June). *The power of vulnerability* [Video]. YouTube. https://www.youtube.com/watch?v=iCvmsMzlF70

- Brown, B. (2010). *TED Talk: The power of vulnerability*. Brené Brown Official Site. https://brenebrown.com/videos/ted-talk-the-power-of-vulnerability/

- Sinek, S. (2009, September). *How great leaders inspire action* [TED Talk]. TEDxPuget Sound. https://www.ted.com/talks/simon_sinek_how_great_leaders_inspire_action

- Sinek, S. (2009). *Start With 'Why' – TED Talk* [Video]. YouTube. https://www.youtube.com/watch?v=2Ss78LfY3nE
- ABC News. (2020, March 24). *Watch and read NSW Premier's coronavirus press conference in full.* https://www.abc.net.au/news/2020-03-24/coronavirus-press-conference-in-full-gladys-berejiklian/12083986
- ABC News. (2020, March 27). *Watch the Premier's full press conference here.* https://www.abc.net.au/news/2020-03-27/nsw-covid-19-full-press-conference/12095810
- National Archives. (n.d.). *Martin Luther King Jr. and the "I Have a Dream" speech.* https://www.archives.gov/press/exhibits/mlk.html
- PBS LearningMedia. (n.d.). *Full text to the "I Have a Dream" speech by Dr. Martin Luther King Jr.* [PDF]. https://static.pbslearningmedia.org/media/media_files/Full_text_I_Have_a_Dream_.pdf

References

- American Rhetoric. (n.d.). *Martin Luther King Jr. – "I Have a Dream" speech.* https://www.americanrhetoric.com/speeches/mlkihaveadream.htm

Chapter 7 – Conflict Resolution

- Nelson Mandela Foundation. (2025, January 27). *Failing South Africa: The Truth Commission 30 years on.* https://www.nelsonmandela.org/news/entry/failing-south-africa-the-truth-commission-30-years-on
- Leadership Story Bank. (2023, November 22). *Nelson Mandela: Truth and Reconciliation.* https://www.leadershipstorybank.com/nelson-mandela-truth-reconciliation/
- Wang, L. Q. (2023). *South Africa establishes a Truth and Reconciliation Commission.* EBSCO Research Starters. https://www.ebsco.com/research-starters/history/south-africa-establishes-truth-and-reconciliation-commission

- Goodwin, D. K. (2005). *Team of rivals: The political genius of Abraham Lincoln*. Simon & Schuster. https://en.wikipedia.org/wiki/Team_of_Rivals
- Gandhi, M. (1961). *Non-violent resistance (Satyagraha)* (B. Kumarappa, Ed.). Schocken Books. https://archive.org/details/nonviolentresist00000gand
- GandhiServe. (n.d.). *The Gandhi Archives*. https://www.gandhiserve.net/gandhiserve-archives/
- Suhrud, T. (Ed.). (2019). *The power of nonviolent resistance: Selected writings*. Penguin Classics. https://www.mkgandhi.org/nbook/power-of-nonviolent-resistance.php
- Knowledge at Wharton. (2018, February 22). *Microsoft CEO Satya Nadella: How empathy sparks innovation*. https://knowledge.wharton.upenn.edu/article/microsofts-ceo-on-how-empathy-sparks-innovation/

References

- IOSR Journal of Business and Management. (2024, December). *Case study: Satya Nadella's leadership at Microsoft.* https://www.iosrjournals.org/iosr-jbm/papers/Vol26-issue12/Ser-2/I2612027479.pdf
- Tribe, L. H. (2013). *Respecting dissent: Justice Ginsburg's critique of the troubling invocation of appearance.* In *Essays in Honor of Justice Ruth Bader Ginsburg.* Harvard Law School. https://dash.harvard.edu/bitstreams/7312037c-d640-6bd4-e053-0100007fdf3b/download
- Boston Public Library. (2020, September 29). *Ruth Bader Ginsburg & dissents: What's a dissent?* https://www.bpl.org/blogs/post/ruth-bader-ginsburg-dissents-whats-a-dissent/

Chapter 8 – Accountability

- Greyser, S. A. (1982). *Johnson & Johnson: The Tylenol Tragedy* [Case study]. Harvard Business School. https://www.hbsp.harvard.edu/product/583043-PDF-ENG

- Irving, L. (2025, November 4). *The impact of Johnson & Johnson's 1982 Tylenol recall on product safety*. California Business Journal. https://calbizjournal.com/the-impact-of-johnson-johnsons-1982-tylenol-recall-on-product-safety/
- National Archives. (n.d.). *General Dwight D. Eisenhower's Order of the Day (1944)*. https://www.archives.gov/milestone-documents/general-eisenhowers-order-of-the-day
- National Archives. (2004). *Eisenhower's Two D-Day Messages*. Prologue Magazine. https://www.archives.gov/publications/prologue/2004/summer/ike-two-d-day-messages
- ESPN News Services. (2018, September 8). *Naomi Osaka wins controversial 2018 US Open; Serena Williams penalized*. ESPN. https://www.espn.com/tennis/story/_/id/24617080/naomi-osaka-wins-controversial-2018-us-open-serena-williams
- Singh, A., Coburn, L., & Rivas, A. (2019, August 15). *Serena Williams outburst at 2018 US Open explored in ESPN's "Backstory"*. ABC

References

News. https://abcnews.go.com/Sports/serena-williams-outburst-2018-us-open-womens-final/story?id=65000510

- Patagonia. (2022, September 14). *Patagonia's next chapter: Earth is now our only shareholder.* Patagonia Works. https://www.patagoniaworks.com/press/2022/9/14/patagonias-next-chapter-earth-is-now-our-only-shareholder

- McCarthy, J. (2022, September 14). *Patagonia founder gives away company so all proceeds can fight climate change.* Global Citizen. https://www.globalcitizen.org/en/content/patagonia-gives-away-company-for-environment/

- Rogers Commission. (1986, June 6). *Report of the Presidential Commission on the Space Shuttle Challenger Accident.* NASA. https://sma.nasa.gov/SignificantIncidents/assets/rogers_commission_report.pdf

- Wikipedia contributors. (n.d.). *Rogers Commission Report.* Wikipedia. https://en.wikipedia.org/wiki/Rogers_Commission_Report

Next-Level Skills

Chapter 9 – Leadership Without Authority

- Verily News. (2025, May 11). *Malala Yousafzai – Global education advocate and inspiration for Nigerian girls' education.* https://verilynews.com/malala-yousafzai-global-education-advocate/
- Vatican News. (2025, September). *Malala: We must all fight courageously for the right to education.* https://www.vaticannews.va/en/world/news/2025-09/malala-yousafzai-women-rights-education-interview.html
- National Archives. (n.d.). *An act of courage: The arrest records of Rosa Parks.* https://www.archives.gov/education/lessons/rosa-parks
- Civil Rights Digital Library. (n.d.). *Montgomery Bus Boycott.* https://crdl.usg.edu/events/montgomery_bus_boycott
- Global Citizen. (2021, August 20). *3 years of Greta Thunberg's activism: How the Swedish*

teenager grew a global climate movement. https://www.globalcitizen.org/en/content/greta-thunberg-climate-action-three-years-movement/

- Fridays for Future. (n.d.). *Fridays for Future – How Greta started a global movement.* https://fridaysforfuture.org/what-we-do/who-we-are/
- The Guardian. (2013, June 9). *Edward Snowden: NSA whistleblower.* https://www.theguardian.com/world/2013/jun/09/edward-snowden-nsa-whistleblower-surveillance
- National Whistleblower Center. (2020, November 19). *The case of Edward Snowden.* https://www.whistleblowers.org/news/the-case-of-edward-snowden/
- Nelson Mandela Foundation. (1998). *Truth and Reconciliation Commission of South Africa Report.* https://www.nelsonmandela.org/uploads/files/TRC-Report-1998.pdf
- BBC News. (1998, October 30). *Desmond Tutu's long crusade.*

http://news.bbc.co.uk/2/hi/special_report/1998/10/98/truth_and_reconciliation/202503.stm

Chapter 10 – Resilience

- NBA.com, "Michael Jordan: Career Retrospective," 2020.
  https://www.nba.com/history/legends/profiles/michael-jordan
- Nike, "Michael Jordan – Failure (Hall of Fame Induction Campaign)," 2006.
  https://news.nike.com/news/michael-jordan-hall-of-fame-failure-commercial
- The New Yorker, "Malcolm Gladwell's Long Road to Mastery," Author Profile Archive, 2015.
  https://www.newyorker.com/contributors/malcolm-gladwell
- Little, Brown and Company, Outliers — Author Notes, 2008.
  https://www.littlebrown.com/titles/malcolm-gladwell/outliers/9780316017930/

References

- ESPN. (2004, January 25). *Surfer girl attacked by shark gets prosthetic arm.* https://www.espn.com/moresports/news/2004/0125/1718320.html
- CNN. (2004, January 13). *Shark victim: 'I shouldn't get special treatment'.* https://www.cnn.com/2004/US/01/13/cnna.hamilton/
- Chesky, B. (2020, March 30). *A letter to hosts.* Airbnb Newsroom. https://news.airbnb.com/a-letter-to-hosts/
- ABC News. (2014, October 10). *Malala Yousafzai wins Nobel Peace Prize for struggle against suppression of children.* https://www.abc.net.au/news/2014-10-10/nobel-peace-prize-satyarthi-yousafzai-win/5805232
- National Women's History Museum. (n.d.). *Biography: Malala Yousafzai.* https://www.womenshistory.org/education-resources/biographies/malala-yousafzai

Chapter 11 – Personal Goal Setting

- Pereira, D. (2025, March 17). *SpaceX Mission and Vision Statement*. Business Model Analyst. https://businessmodelanalyst.com/spacex-mission-and-vision-statement/
- Parker, B. (2025, March 13). *SpaceX Mission Statement | Vision | Core Values | Strategy*. Business Strategy Hub. https://bstrategyhub.com/spacex-mission-statement-vision-core-values-analysis/
- Ford, B. D. (2019, May 28). *French Open 2019 – Serena Williams fights through sluggish start to win opener*. ESPN. https://www.espn.ph/tennis/story/_/id/26833144/french-open-2019-serena-williams-fights-sluggish-start-win-opener
- Gates, B., & Gates, M. (2020, February 10). *2020 Annual Letter: Why we swing for the fences*. Gates Notes. https://www.gatesnotes.com/2020-Annual-Letter
- Gates Foundation. (n.d.). *Gates Foundation Annual Letters*.

https://www.gatesfoundation.org/ideas/annual-letters
- GazeOUT. (2023, November 17). *Oprah's Vision Board Success Story.* https://gazeout.com/oprahs-vision-board-success-story
- BBC Sport. (2018, January 28). *Australian Open 2018 men's final: Roger Federer beats Marin Cilic.* https://www.bbc.com/sport/live/tennis/42444933/page/2
- Wikipedia contributors. (n.d.). *2018 Roger Federer tennis season.* Wikipedia. https://en.wikipedia.org/wiki/2018_Roger_Federer_tennis_season

Chapter 12 – Storytelling for Influence

- Jobs, S. (2007, January 9). *Steve Jobs Keynote – First iPhone Presentation.* MacWorld Conference. [YouTube Video]. https://www.youtube.com/watch?v=2MlSJLPxGYs

- Singju Post. (2014, July 4). *Steve Jobs iPhone 2007 Presentation (Full Transcript)*. https://singjupost.com/steve-jobs-iphone-2007-presentation-full-transcript/
- Eadicicco, L. (2017, January 9). *Watch Steve Jobs Launch the iPhone at Apple's 2007 Keynote*. TIME. https://time.com/4628515/steve-jobs-iphone-launch-keynote-2007/
- National Archives. (n.d.). *Martin Luther King Jr. and the "I Have a Dream" Speech*. https://www.archives.gov/press/exhibits/mlk.html
- PBS LearningMedia. (n.d.). *Full Text: "I Have a Dream" Speech by Dr. Martin Luther King Jr.* [PDF]. https://static.pbslearningmedia.org/media/media_files/Full_text_I_Have_a_Dream_.pdf
- American Rhetoric. (n.d.). *Martin Luther King Jr. – "I Have a Dream" Speech*. https://www.americanrhetoric.com/speeches/mlkihaveadream.htm
- Sandberg, S., & Grant, A. (2017). *Option B: Facing adversity, building resilience, and*

References

finding joy. Knopf. https://www.penguin.com.au/books/option-b-9780753548295

- OptionB.org. (n.d.). *About the Book – Option B*. https://optionb.org/book
- The Atlantic. (2017, January 19). *The Story of an Iconic Obama Campaign Chant, Animated*. https://www.theatlantic.com/video/index/513629/fired-up-ready-to-go/
- Gupta-Carlson, H. (2016). *Re-Imagining the Nation: Storytelling and Social Media in the Obama Campaigns*. Cambridge University Press. https://www.cambridge.org/core/journals/ps-political-science-and-politics/article/reimagining-the-nation-storytelling-and-social-media-in-the-obama-campaigns/21504D31A0D6F1588E6CF529003D0BA6
- Brown, B. (2010, June). *The Power of Vulnerability* [TED Talk]. TEDxHouston. https://www.ted.com/talks/brene_brown_the_power_of_vulnerability

- Brown, B. (2010, June). *TED Talk: The Power of Vulnerability*. Brené Brown Official Site. https://brenebrown.com/videos/ted-talk-the-power-of-vulnerability/

Chapter 13 – Integration: Bringing It All Together

- Harvard Business Publishing. (2023). *The future of human-centric leadership: 2023 global leadership development study*. Harvard Business Publishing. https://www.harvardbusiness.org/insight/2023-global-leadership-development-study/
- Hayward, A. (2022, December 5). *Training soft skills at scale is the key to transformation success*. Chief Learning Officer. https://www.chieflearningofficer.com/2022/12/05/training-soft-skills-at-scale-is-the-key-to-transformation-success/
- Gallo, C. (2021, October 5). *The skills that define modern leaders*. Forbes. https://www.forbes.com/sites/carminegallo/2

021/10/05/the-skills-that-define-modern-leaders/
- McKinsey & Company. (n.d.). *Soft skills for a hard world*. McKinsey & Company. https://www.mckinsey.com/featured-insights/future-of-work/five-fifty-soft-skills-for-a-hard-world

Next-Level Skills

Index

*Below is a thematic index of key ideas, concepts, and examples referenced throughout **Next-Level Skills***

A – C

Accountability – Chapter 8; personal ownership, integrity, trust, NASA's Challenger response, Patagonia's purpose-driven model, p. 221.

Active Listening – Chapter 3; empathy, attention, Barack Obama, Brené Brown, Indra Nooyi, p. 79.

Adaptability – Chapter 4; flexibility, mindset, Netflix reinvention, Jacinda Ardern's leadership, p. 109.

Albert Einstein – Chapter 6; clarity and simplicity in communication, p. 165.

Authenticity – Chapters 3, 6 & 12; Brené Brown, Indra Nooyi, vulnerability as influence, pp. 79, 165, 333.

Awareness (Self-) – Chapter 1; mindfulness, inner reflection, Satya Nadella, Oprah Winfrey, p. 21.

D – F

Decision-Making – Chapter 5; strategic foresight, Jeff Bezos, Steve Jobs, long-term planning, p. 137.

Discipline – Chapters 8 & 11; consistent habits, Serena Williams, Bill Gates, pp. 221, 307.

Emotional Intelligence (EI) – Chapter 2; empathy, emotional regulation, Jacinda Ardern, Michelle Obama, p. 51.

Empathy – Chapters 2, 6 & 7; Satya Nadella's leadership, Simon Sinek, cross-cultural understanding, pp. 51, 165, 195.

Feedback – Chapters 3 & 8; constructive dialogue, learning mindset, pp. 79, 221.

Flexibility – Chapter 4; growth mindset, embracing change, leadership adaptability, p. 109.

G – I

Grit – Chapters 10 & 11; resilience under challenge, Roger Federer, Bethany Hamilton, pp. 281, 307.

Growth Mindset – Chapters 1 & 4; Ray Dalio, J.K. Rowling, pp. 21, 109.

Goals (Personal) – Chapter 11; clarity of intention, Elon Musk, Oprah Winfrey, Roger Federer, p. 307.

Habits – Chapters 8 & 11; Atomic Habits, small wins, behaviour change, pp. 221, 307.

Index

Influence – Chapters 9 & 12; leadership through story, Martin Luther King Jr., Steve Jobs, Malala Yousafzai, pp. 249, 333.

Integrity – Chapters 8 & 9; moral leadership, accountability, Desmond Tutu, pp. 221, 249.

J – M

Jacinda Ardern – Chapters 2; empathy in leadership, clarity in crisis, pp. 51.

Jeff Bezos – Chapter 5; long-term thinking, strategic patience, p. 137.

J.K. Rowling – Chapter 4; perseverance through rejection, creative resilience, p. 109.

Leadership – All chapters; influence, self-awareness, integrity, communication, see entire book.

Listening – Chapter 3; Barack Obama, Dalai Lama, active listening practices, p. 79.

Malala Yousafzai – Chapters 2, 9 & 10; moral courage, advocacy for education, pp. 51, 249, 281.

Mandela, Nelson – Chapters 3 & 7; active listening, reconciliation, resilience, moral strength, pp. 79, 195.

Mindset – Chapters 1 & 4; adaptability, self-awareness, learning orientation, pp. 21, 109.

N – R

Nadella, Satya – Chapters 1, 2 & 7; empathy-driven transformation at Microsoft, pp. 21, 51, 195.

Netflix – Chapter 4; strategic adaptability in business, p. 109.

Nooyi, Indra – Chapters 3; empathetic communication and listening, pp. 79.

Oprah Winfrey – Chapters 1 & 11; authenticity, intention, self-awareness, pp. 21, 307.

Patagonia – Chapter 8; accountability to purpose and planet, p. 221.

Purpose – Chapters 5, 8, & 11; vision, accountability, sustainability, pp. 137, 221, 307.

Resilience – Chapter 10; Micheal Jordan, Bethany Hamilton, Airbnb recovery, p. 281.

Ruth Bader Ginsburg – Chapter 7; respectful dissent, empathy in conflict, p. 195.

S – T

Sandberg, Sheryl – Chapters 5 & 12; vulnerability and resilience, pp. 137, 333.

Self-Awareness – Chapter 1; introspection, feedback, emotional literacy, p. 21.

Serena Williams – Chapters 1, 4, 8 & 11; discipline, accountability, self-reflection, pp. 21, 109, 221, 307.

Sharma, Robin – Chapter 9; The Leader Who Had No Title, p. 249.

Sinek, Simon – Chapters 6 & 12; purpose-driven leadership, Start with Why, pp. 165, 333.

Storytelling – Chapter 12; communication, narrative influence, connection, p. 333.

Strategic Thinking – Chapter 5; foresight, systems thinking, purpose alignment, p. 137.

U – Z

Viktor Frankl – Chapter 10; meaning in adversity, pp. 281.

Vulnerability – Chapters 2 & 12; Brené Brown, authenticity in influence, pp. 51, 333.

Winfrey, Oprah – Chapters 1 & 11; emotional intelligence, vision, and clarity, pp. 21, 307.

Zig Ziglar – Chapter 11; goal-setting wisdom, p. 307.

www.ingramcontent.com/pod-product-compliance
Lightning Source LLC
Chambersburg PA
CBHW071948070526
44583CB00015B/1105